Adept Circle
Magick

TO JAN —

It has been my pleasure
to meet & talk with you.
Good luck in your growth &
education.

Blessings,

K.L.

Adept Circle Magick

A Guide for the Advanced Wiccan Practitioner

KIRK WHITE

CITADEL PRESS
Kensington Publishing Corp.
www.kensingtonbooks.com

To the primary women in my life:
Amy, Killian, and Diane.

CITADEL PRESS BOOKS are published by

Kensington Publishing Corp.
850 Third Avenue
New York, NY 10022

All Kensington titles, imprints, and distributed lines are available at special quantity discounts for bulk purchases for sales promotions, premiums, fund-raising, educational, or institutional use. Special book excerpts or customized printings can also be created to fit specific needs. For details, write or phone the office of the Kensington special sales manager: Kensington Publishing Corp., 850 Third Avenue, New York, NY 10022, attn: Special Sales Department; phone: 1-800-221-2647.

CITADEL PRESS and the Citadel logo are Reg. U.S. Pat. & TM Off.

First printing: April 2006

10 9 8 7 6 5 4 3 2 1

Printed in the United States of America

Library of Congress Control Number: 2005934019

ISBN 0-8065-2699-8

CONTENTS

Adepthood and Life After Wicca 101

Picture yourself in the future. After a long, hard struggle you have finally "made it." You have attained everything in life that you have always wanted—the knowledge, the confidence, the respect, and even the material things that you've dreamed of. You have complete mastery over your life and your life has become a masterpiece. How does that feel? What does it look like? What kinds of skills, knowledge, and personality traits have you developed to get to this position?

"Adept" is a word with many connotations, associations, and meanings. Technically, the word simply means "one who has attained," referring to mastery over some area of knowledge. The area of knowledge can be anything from quantum physics to shooting jump shots. In this particular case, we are talking about mastery over your own life—the ability to become that person you dream of.

You might ask: "What does this have to do with circle magick?" The answer to this question is multilayered. First, on the most superficial level, the answer is that as Wiccans most of our magickal workings are done in a ritual circle. Since all the topics covered in the book often take place in magick circles, then this is "circle magick."

Second, as a beginning Wiccan practitioner, most students are gradually introduced to the main areas of study: basic magick skills, creating sacred space, energy work, divination, the ritual calendar, initiation, working with deity, and personal growth and transformation. We start out knowing little or nothing and are taught a few basics in each area. Once we have those mastered, we are taught the next level of each. As we evolve and grow, we gradually see how each area is intertwined with the others. Thus, our learning process is not linear. We don't learn all there is to know about divination before learning about energy work. We don't get all of our initiations and then learn about ritual spaces. Thus, our learning is circular and spiraling.

We go around the circle of knowledge learning a little of each, with the preceding area of study providing some skills and knowledge that will help us master the next area. Some of the basic skills and concepts learned in divination can help when it comes to the ritual calendar. However, until we have a larger picture of how each of the areas fit together and we have done the personal growth work, we can't move to the next deeper level of each. We have to go entirely around the circle of skills once before we can move on to the next level. Each turn around the circle spirals us closer to full mastery of circle magick.

Lastly, two definitions of "circle" are: "the area within which something or someone exerts influence" and "a series ending where it began, especially when perpetually repeated." As living beings, we are active participants in the circle of life. And whether we accept it or not, our lives are the only area where we exert influence. As Wiccans and Pagans, we know that all life is magick. We know that by attuning ourselves to the ebbs and flows of nature, by opening our awareness to how energy works in the world, and by working with the Divine Will we are doing magick. Thus, circle magick also refers to how we recognize and use magick in our daily lives. Circle magick *is* our daily lives.

So, when we talk about "adept circle magick" we are referring to three different levels:

1. Mastery of the skills and knowledge of those things typically done in magick circles
2. Mastery of how each of those skill areas fits together and interacts at a deep level
3. Mastery of ourselves and our lives

By accomplishing the first two, we attain the skills to accomplish the third, becoming adept at creating the very life—the masterpiece—that we imagined during the beginning exercise.

This book is designed to help you become that adept. It is a product of over thirty years of study, practice, and searching. Although it focuses on Wicca, the concepts and exercises are drawn from years of study and practice in several branches of Paganism—from Druidry to Reconstructionist to various kinds of Witchcraft. Also tied in are experiences and insights drawn from such diverse areas as Buddhist and Taoist meditation, Pentacostal trance and "slaying in the Spirit," Vodoun, Chinese medicine, parapsychological research, transpersonal psychology, ceremonial magick, the qabalah, mediumship, faery work, and plain old folk magick and wisdom.

The book is comprised of eight chapters, with each representing a different area of study and work in Wiccan practice. It begins with chapter 1, which focuses on basic magickal skills such as how magickal energy is raised and flows and how various ritual movements, postures, breathing, and mental states affect the quantity and quality of the energy raised.

The basics of energy flow are followed by chapter 2, which discusses creating ritual spaces. Here, the newly developed energy skills can be combined with deeper insights into how ritual spaces are influenced by shape and intent to create spaces customized to the ritual intent of the practitioner.

The ability to create appropriate ritual spaces then sets the backdrop for advanced divination in chapter 3. In this chapter, the reader learns to develop his or her intuition and clairvoyance for use in everything from deciding on a ritual format to questions in daily living.

Skill in intuitively picking up the subtle energies and influences of the Divine and the natural world around us easily flows in chapter 4 into an exploration of the cycles of nature and how we can work with them symbolically and ritually to better align ourselves with it.

Chapter 5 provides the opportunity to combine one's skill in basic energy work, creation of sacred space, intuition and divination, and awareness of nature's cycles with advanced work in healing and spellworking. Here, the magickal work acquires a practical edge.

Most readers of this book have probably experienced one or more initiations. However, as advanced practitioners, we become aware that every day is a new initiation of some kind. By taking the skills covered in the previous chapters and combining them with a deeper understanding of the different types, styles, intents, and effects of various initiation rites, mastery of chapter 6 provides an opportunity to craft highly effective transformative initiations for oneself and others.

Chapter 7 delves into the powerful work of divine possession. "Drawing Down the Moon," also known as "aspecting" or "divine possession," is mentioned in several introductory books. However, since most covens reserve this powerful work for higher-level practitioners, very little is in print as to the specific types, levels, or techniques of divine possession in a Wiccan context. Discussion of the various theological models common in Wicca, the various levels of possession, techniques for invoking divine possession on oneself or another, the ethics of doing so, and how to care for someone while and after he or she is possessed are covered.

Finally, chapter 8 brings all the insights, knowledge, and experiences of the preceding chapters back to the main question of how to translate the skills of being adept in one's magickal circle to becoming adept in the greater circle of one's own life.

In martial arts practice, it is often said that a person could attain complete mastery of the art by just focusing on the very first lesson he or she receives and that a true master is always going back to those early lessons to find the insights he or she missed before. The same applies to becoming adept at circle magick. Chapter 8 integrates the first spiral around the wheel of Wiccan knowledge presented in this book, but it is just the beginning. Once you have finished the book, it is time to begin again at chapter 1 and the basics where new insights and knowledge can still be found. Adepthood is not a destination, but a never-ending journey of personal growth and transformation. Thus 'round the circle doth turn and the spiral continues.

Each chapter in *Adept Circle Magick* includes a number of training exercises, rituals, and invocations. These kinds of magickal workings are usually closely held by the traditions of origin with all members being bound by solemn oaths of secrecy. In order to not violate any of these oaths, all the exercises, rituals, and invocations in this book are original compositions unless they are so much in the open domain that trying to keep them secret becomes absurd. A well-read and/or experienced practitioner will recognize elements of several traditions in each, but all have been altered from the original. Those in this book have been inspired or influenced by a wide variety of traditions and groups, but they do not represent the teachings or practices of any one particular tradition.

Furthermore, each of the rituals, prayers, meditations, and invocations have been written in a generic form, omitting such things as specific names of deity and elemental correspondences whenever possible, so that they can easily be modified by practitioners to fit their own styles, beliefs, and practices. The goal of this book is not to teach people how to be "our" kind of Wiccan, but to help people to better understand and build their own Wiccan practice.

There are times when this book may seem more like a textbook than a traditional book on Wiccan practice. This book is the first of a two-book combination. *Adept Circle Magick* lays the major theoretical groundwork, providing just enough exercises, rituals, and spellworkings to introduce the ideas and give you a taste of what such practices could be like. The second book, *Adept Rites and Spells*, provides an expanded catalog of exercises, spells, meditations, and rituals in each of the areas addressed in *Adept Circle Magick*. Together, *Adept Circle Magick* and *Adept Rites and Spells* comprise a fully developed system of training and resources to support the intermediate and advanced Wiccan practitioner in his or her growth toward full magickal mastery.

ACKNOWLEDGMENTS

This book has been a long time coming. I'd like to thank the following people without whom my first book would never have been:

Cat Chapin-Bishop, Doug Nelson, Maureen Reddington-Wilde, Kathy Perine, and my other spiritual siblings from the Church of the Sacred Earth. Those twenty-five years of long discussions on the nature and method of magick and spiritual practice form the backbone of this book.

Judy Harrow and Laura Wildman-Hanlon, who encouraged me to send in my first book proposal. They even connected me to their, and now my, literary agent Jennie Dunham.

Jennie Dunham, who held my hand and gently shepherded me through the process of getting my first book contract.

Bob Shuman, my editor at Kensington Publishing. Bob exerted the right amount of encouragement, cajoling, insight, suggestions, and pressure to help make this book the best it could be.

Dr. Diane Johnson, editor, business manager, advisor, coach, biggest cheerleader, and very dear friend. Words cannot begin to express how critical she's been to this process and my life.

My wife, Amy, and our daughter, Killian. They are the bedrock on which my life is built. Their love and understanding sustained me during those long days and nights at the keyboard.

My communities at Laurelin Community, Covenant of the Goddess, and Cherry Hill Seminary, who have been my test cases, sounding boards, and supporters.

All the Pagans around the country whom I've met in my travels who encouraged me and supported me in writing this book.

Thank you all.

CHAPTER 1

Touching Ground:
Reaffirming the Basics

You are a witch. You are powerful and creative. As the saying goes, you are "beloved among Gods and men." This book has been written precisely for you—the intermediate or advanced Wiccan practitioner who is seeking to expand and deepen your skills and knowledge. You are seeking adepthood.

One of the foundational qualities of an adept is a high level of skill in magick. Because of your previous mastery of beginning Wicca, you should already know how to raise magickal energy and how to move, manipulate, and use it. However, as we move deeper into magick, we will also be working with the stronger, wilder forces of nature. Therefore, it is imperative that you have all the basic skills perfected and consistent. In many ways, magick is like working with electricity. With electricity, if you are working with it at low voltage and make a mistake, it might sting a bit but you'll live. At higher voltages, the chance of serious harm becomes higher and thus you need to be more consistent and careful when working with it. The same is true with magick. As such, an aspiring adept must also make sure that his or her knowledge of magickal working is rock solid and his or her performance is carefully considered and consistent.

At the very least, just as with the martial arts, it does not matter how advanced a person is. Everyone can always benefit from

1

review of the fundamentals, either because there is just so much
to learn that no one person can ever really master it all, or because now, having a more advanced perspective, you may notice
something overlooked before.

Magick: A Definition

Since the primary focus of this chapter is on how to develop
one's magickal abilities, it makes sense to define what magick is.
For the purposes of this book, we will distinguish between ritual
magick or magickal operations, such as spells, and magickal
living.

Ritual magick is the art and science of developing and changing your consciousness to be aware of the natural forces affecting
you and the world around you. By making these changes and becoming aware of these forces, you can then manipulate them to
achieve further spiritual growth and effect changes in your physical environment. To put it another way, by developing your magickal abilities such as will and imagination, will can then be directed
by imagination in accord with the laws of nature to manifest real
change in your self and world. A simple, mundane example of
this would be that by becoming aware of how your local political
process works, you can then get involved and affect who runs for
office and gets elected. Magickally, if you are aware of how the
moon's energy affects people's moods, you can then plan events
and activities to capitalize on it. For example, when the moon is
in Taurus, and knowing that people are generally more likely to
be looking for romantic relationships at that time, you might choose
that night as the best time for a first date or to do spellworking
around finding a mate.

Magickal living is very similar but with a major distinction.
Magickal living involves developing your magickal abilities and
consciousness so that you can better attune yourself to the flow of

nature, its cycles and energies, so that you are fully in synchronization with the Will of the Divine. Once you are so attuned, you are living magickally.

The major distinction between magickal living and ritual magick, then, is that magickal living is not something you do like ritual magick, but something to be. Magickal adepts know how to do ritual magick, but seldom have to because they are living magickally. That is, if you are in tune with the Will of the Divine and the energies around you, everything in your life should be going peacefully and harmoniously so that you do not have to do magick. It is when you stop being magickal and lose your attunement that you have to do ritual magick to rectify things.

The Three Basic Skills

There are three basic sets of skills or abilities that any student of magickal work must have if he or she wants to be successful in his or her studies and workings. They prepare you for the work ahead and ensure that the magickal work that you do will be safe and balanced. These three are the abilities to:

- Relax and meditate
- Ground and center
- Create sacred/safe space

Relaxation and Meditation

The ability to relax deeply is a prerequisite for most magickal and spiritual work. The body, due to stress, diet, and injuries, often has several areas of holding where the muscles are tight or we protect by never allowing ourselves to relax. For many people, it is the shoulders, neck, and head area.

If a body holds and stores tension for a long time, it eventually starts assuming that the restricted tight nature of the area is normal and we become unconscious of these areas or we develop chronic conditions such as migraine headaches and back pain. Thus, from a strictly health perspective, deep relaxation is very important to everyone.

Magickally, it is important for three reasons. First, wherever there is holding, it is holding more than just tension. It is holding energy. Thus, when a person with a lot of tension tries to do magick, he or she is unable to access and use the energy stores available and his or her spellworking will be correspondingly less effective. Only when energy is free flowing does it work most efficiently. As an adept, you will need to raise large amounts of energy; as such, any blockages you have will have to be removed. Second, relaxation removes the pain and distractions associated with the body, allowing for greater focus, more vivid imagination, and deeper trance work. It quiets the mind of distracting thoughts, thus leaving it open to receiving intuition and Divine inspiration. As you will see in later chapters, working with intuition and Divine inspiration are major parts of an adept's training and magickal working, so again, relaxation can play a larger role in preparing you for this work. Third, meditation as a regular discipline is an excellent technique for building one's magickal will. Later in this chapter, we will discuss the importance of building your magickal will, but the main point is that magick requires the development of self-discipline. So if you are going to have to discipline yourself to do something regularly anyway, it might as well be relaxation and meditation.

Meditation can take many different forms but has essentially two main purposes: to quiet the mind of all thoughts and to focus the mind on a particular symbol or set of symbols. Both ultimately lead to insight into one's self and/or situation. By quieting your mind, you open yourself up to noticing things you might not have before and make room for the possibility that intuition or Divine inspiration might happen. By focusing your mind on a specific symbol, particularly one with many different layers of associations and meanings, your mind is led into other pathways of thinking, making connections you might not have otherwise, and again, opening up the possibility for intuition or inspiration to happen.

Basic Skills Exercise 1: Relaxation and Rainbow Meditation

The purpose of this exercise is to induce deep, full body relaxation and focus the mind on various energies or aspects within the body as represented by the colors of the rainbow. You may find it useful to record this meditation and then play it back so that you can concentrate fully on the imagery.

Begin by loosening your clothes so that nothing is tight or binds. Lie down on the floor or a bed or sit in a chair. Try to be comfortable but not so much that you'll fall asleep. Close your eyes and take a few deep breaths—breathing in through your nose and out through your mouth. Breath in. Breath out. Breath in. Breath out. Clear your mind of any distracting thoughts. Lay any thoughts or worries aside for now, knowing that they will still be there when you come back. But for now, just focus on your deep, slow breathing—in and out, in and out. As you breathe, feel the tension gradually drain out from your body. With every out breath goes tension. With every in breath comes warmth and relaxation. Out goes tension, in comes relaxation. And as you become more and more relaxed, you start to feel in your body a warm sensation and a gentle vibration, filling you with warmth and relaxation. A warm sensation . . . a gentle vibration leaving you feeling warm and relaxed.

Gradually, focus your attention on your feet. Tighten your feet briefly and then let them relax. And as you breathe, feel all tension draining out of your feet and feel them becoming filled with that warm sensation—that gentle vibration—leaving them warm and relaxed.

Then move your attention up to your calves. Tighten your calves briefly and then let them relax. And as you breathe, feel all tension draining out of your calves and feel them becoming filled with that warm sensation—that gentle vibration—leaving them warm and relaxed.

Then move your attention up to your knees and the backs of your knees. Tighten your knees briefly and then let them relax. And as you breathe, feel all tension draining out of your knees and feel them becoming filled with that warm sensation—that gentle vibration—leaving them warm and relaxed.

Then move your attention up to your thighs. Tighten your thighs briefly and then let them relax. And as you breathe, feel all tension draining out of your thighs and feel them becoming filled with that warm sensation—that gentle vibration—leaving them warm and relaxed.

Tighten your groin and buttocks and let them relax. Feel the warmth and gentle vibration move up into your groin and buttocks, leaving them warm and relaxed.

Feel the warm vibration move up into your lower back and up your sides. With every breath you feel the tension draining out of your lower back and sides, leaving them warm and relaxed.

Feel the warm vibration move up into your upper back and chest. With every breath you feel the tension draining out of your upper back and chest, leaving them warm and relaxed. Warm and relaxed.

Feel the warm vibration move up your arms and out into your hands. Briefly tighten your arms, hands, and fingers and then let the tension go, draining away with every out breath. Leaving you with that warm sensation and gentle vibration feeling very, very relaxed.

Feel the warm vibration move in to your shoulders and neck. Briefly tighten your shoulders and neck and then let the tension go, draining away with every out breath. Leaving you with that warm sensation and gentle vibration feeling very, very relaxed.

Finally, feel the warm vibration move up into your face—across your cheeks, into your lips and nose, into all the small muscles around your eyes and your temples, around the back of your head and up to the top. Briefly make your face and head muscles as tight as possible and then relax and with every breath feel the tension draining away, leaving them with that warm sensation and gentle vibration, feeling very, very relaxed.

You are now fully relaxed and ready to begin the rainbow meditation.

Picture in your mind the color red. You can do this by picturing something red like an apple or as if you are looking through glasses with red lenses. See the color red. Then feel it filling your whole body so that you are filled with and radiating red light. Bathe in the red light for a while and feel your body. Red is the color of the body's inner fire and of healing. Feel the red light healing and enlivening your body.

Now picture the color orange. Either see in your mind something orange like a ball or the fruit or as if you are looking through glasses with orange-colored lenses. See orange. Feel it filling your body and radiating from it, and be aware of your emotions right now. Orange is the color of emotions.

Now picture the color yellow. Either picture a yellow object such as a bright yellow raincoat or see things as if you are looking through yellow-colored lenses. See yellow and feel it filling your body and your mind. Yellow is the color of thoughts and the mind.

Now picture the color green. Either picture something green such as grass or imagine looking through green-colored lenses. See green and feel it filling your whole body and giving it nourishment and substance. You feel very safe. Green is the color of nourishment, safety, and being grounded.

Now picture the color blue. Either picture something blue such as the sky or ocean or imagine seeing things as if you are looking through blue-colored lenses. See blue and feel it filling your whole body. Feel it radiating out from you in rays going out to touch all the

*people you love. And feel their blue rays of love coming back to you.
Blue is the color of love.*

*Now picture the color indigo (dark blue). Either picture something
indigo such as the night sky or imagine seeing things as if you are
looking through indigo-colored lenses. See indigo filling your whole
body and see and feel your dreams and aspirations. Indigo is the
color of aspirations toward growth.*

*Now picture the color purple. Either picture something purple or
imagine looking through purple-colored lenses. See purple and feel
it filling your whole body. Feel yourself connected to some higher
source of guidance or inspiration. Purple is the color of inspiration.*

*Now gradually picture the colors in reverse order . . . purple . . .
indigo . . . blue . . . green . . . yellow . . . orange . . . and red. Then
gradually feel yourself in your body. Become aware of the feel of the
floor or chair under you. Become aware of the room and the sounds
around you. Remain still for a while and when you are ready, gradually open your eyes and sit up. You are back.*

Grounding and Centering

Grounding is the process of making a connection, energetically
if not actually, with the earth or ground. It provides a solid foundation from whence to commence any magickal operation and a
place to put any leftover or unwanted energy. When we show up
for a ritual after having dealt with the mundane world of house,
car, job, family, and neighbors, it is important that we make a
break from any thoughts or emotions that may be lingering from
our earlier interactions, especially if they were negative in any
way. The last thing we want to do is bring our anger from being
cut off in traffic on our way to circle *into* the circle. So we need to
ground our energies and clear our minds.

Grounding also allows you to draw some of your magickal energy from the earth rather than using only your own and becoming depleted. It also serves as a sort of lightning rod through
which energies, either those left over from magick workings or

sent in from somewhere else, can be safely conducted to the ground rather than burning out your mind and body. As an adept who will be working with higher-voltage energy, the ability to ground is crucial. I have known Pagans who have developed severe physical and mental health problems from working with too much energy and not adequately grounding it from their bodies. So be forewarned.

Centering is the process of aligning yourself with the universe. It is the process of "being here now," of finding your psychic or energetic center of gravity, so to speak. When you center, as the name implies, you want to make it so that you are centered on both the vertical and horizontal axes. That is, vertically you want to place yourself so that your head is up toward the sky and the base of your spine is down toward the earth. This creates a situation where you are a balanced channel between earth and sky energies. Horizontally, you are trying to place yourself at the imaginary center of all directions. You are not leaning forward or back, left or right. Instead, your body is upright and equidistant from the ends of the infinite universe. By doing this, you bring your focus to the center of your being, and at the same time align your center with the center of the universe so that all thoughts or insights that arise while you are in your centered place are in tune with the wisdom and knowledge of the Divine. You are essentially sighting yourself—your will, imagination, and awareness— at the crosshairs of the universe where there is infinite possibility.

Basic Skills Exercise 2: Grounding and Centering

Sit comfortably on the floor or if preferable, directly on the ground. Close your eyes and feel the connection between your buttocks and base of your spine against the ground. Feel the solidity and support of the earth. Feel how heavy your body feels against it.

Now feel your spine sinking down into the earth like a pole or roots. Feel it moving deeper and deeper into the ground, strengthening your connection and support. And into the roots or pole feel energy move up from the earth with every in breath, filling you with energy and making you calm and steady. With every out breath, feel the energy pour back down the pole or roots and out into the earth. Do this for several minutes.

When you are ready and feel fully grounded, try to get a sense of your body posture and position with regard to right and left. Get a sense of what is straight up and centered—not leaning to one side or the other. Feel your center of gravity, both physically and psychically. You are now grounded and centered.

Basic Skills Exercise 3: The Qabalistic Cross

Another commonly used technique that both grounds and centers is the Ritual of the Qabalistic Cross. There are several variations on this ritual, but here is a version that seems to work very well.

Begin facing East, the direction of wisdom, knowledge, and enlightenment. With feet at shoulder width apart, start by taking several deep breaths. If you are working in a group, try to synchronize your breathing, movements, and intonations during this entire ritual. While breathing, your hands are extended down, palms down toward the Earth. Focus your imagination on reaching deep into the core of the Earth and grasping the energy of the Goddess.

Reach up with your hands as far as you can reach. Stretch your arms and hands toward the sky. Envision your hands reaching up beyond the stars, beyond the dark edges of the universe, to the Divine spark that became the manifest world. When you grasp that spark, bring your hands together, still extended over your head, into the shape of a triangle with the point upward—the symbol of Fire. Slowly bring this triangle down to your third eye while intoning the word

"ATAH" [pronounced ah-tah *and means "thou art"]. Envision the Light of the Divine extending down to and shining forth from your third eye.*

Take a deep breath and with your hands still in the Fire triangle form, start to bring them down in front of your body. At the level of your heart, flip your hands over so that now the point of the triangle is downward—the symbol of Water. Keep extending your hands downward until about the level of your groin, where they will naturally reach their limit and pull apart. All during this downward motion of your hands, from forehead to groin, intone the word "MALKUTH" [pronounced mahl-koot and means "the kingdom"]. During this process, envision the Light running down through the center of your body into the ground and eventually reaching the very center of the Earth. What you have done so far is to connect Heaven and Earth with yourself as the channel and conduit between the two. You are now grounded and centered in an up-down axis.

With your hands still in the downward position, start to inhale and then bring them back together and up to your heart level. At the heart level, extend your right arm and hand all the way to the right. Your hand should be in a closed fist position, which symbolizes severity and limitation. During this extension, see your arm extending all the way to the right to the corners of the Universe and intone the word "VE GEBURAH" [pronounced vay-ge-boo-rah and means "the power"]. With your inhalation, bring your right hand back to your heart while envisioning that you are also bringing that link to the corner of the Universe back into your heart.

Now extend your left arm and hand all the way to the left. Your hand should be open and your palm open in a position of mercy and openness, the counterweight to severity and limitation. During this extension, envision your arm extending all the way to the left to the corners of the Universe and intone the word "VE GEDULAH" [pronounced vay-ge-doo-lah and means "the glory"]. With the inhale, bring your left hand back to your heart while envisioning that you are also bringing that link to the corner of the Universe back into your heart.

Now open your arms wide as if you are going to give someone a big hug and bring your hands all the way back around and together at your heart. During this process, imagine yourself bringing in all the connections and energy of nature and, when you finally press your hands to your chest, sealing those connections into your heart. The word to intone is "LE OLAM" [pronounced lay-oh-lahm and means "forever"]. Draw out the final "m" sound at the end.

After one final deep inhale, drop your hands back to your sides and the Ritual of the Qabalistic Cross is finished.

Creating Sacred Space: Basic Circle Casting

In beginning and intermediate Wicca, almost every magickal operation is done within sacred space in the shape of a circle. The two main purposes of casting one are to contain the energy generated within the circle until it is willfully released for a particular purpose and to protect the inhabitants of the circle from unwanted or harmful energies or influences. The circle is also keenly involved in the symbolism revolving around the four elements, the cycles of the year, and other mythic structures in Wiccan practice. We will get into this in much greater detail later. For now, as a preliminary working, we are primarily interested in the circle's protective qualities.

Basic Skills Exercise 4: Casting a Basic Protective Circle

After grounding and centering, take a moment to stand quietly in the center of where you are going to be doing your ritual. Conjure in your mind the image of a vibrant, almost electrical blue flame. When you are ready, walk to the edge of where you are going to trace your circle. Direct your forefinger and middle finger to the edge of your ritual space. Then visualize that electrical blue flame shooting out of the tips of your fingers to the edge of the circle, where it spreads out creating a protective barrier between you and the rest of the world. Walk around the perimeter of your circle, projecting the magickal fire out to create a circle of blue flame around you. Notice that the blue flame isn't just a vertical wall, but curls upward over your head to create a dome. Imagine the flame is doing likewise down into the floor or ground where you cannot see it, creating a ball of protective blue flame with you inside of that ball. Once you have completely circled your space, closing up the entire space, visualize the blue flame ceasing to shoot out of your fingers while the blue circle around you remains. You are now in a magickal circle.

When you are done with whatever work you want to do in the circle, reverse the process you went through to create it. Walk in the reverse direction around the edge of the circle holding your right hand out with palm open like a giant scoop. As you walk around slowly, visualize your hand drawing in and scooping up all the blue magickal fire. Once you have completed circling your space and have scooped up the entire blue flaming ball, place your hands on the floor and visualize the magickal fire pouring out of you and into the earth. When all of the blue flame is gone, you are done.

The Four Magickal Abilities

The four magickal abilities are commonly known in Wiccan practice. In some traditions, they are also called the Witches' Pyramid, each ability being represented by one side of the pyramid. When combined, they form the foundation and sides of the pyramid and culminate at the peak as adepthood. Although we'll soon be discussing them more fully, these abilities are:

- To will
- To dare
- To know
- To keep silent

To Will: The Magickal Will

People tend to think of the will as simply the focused desire and commitment to make something happen. However, in reality there are three types of will. They are:

- The strong will
- The skillful will
- The higher will

The strong will is the one we usually think of when we hear the word "will." It is that intense desire and commitment to have or do something. When we talk about someone not having enough willpower to do something, we are talking about strong will. It is the ability to focus and work single-mindedly on a desired outcome until it comes true.

There are many exercises published on how to build your strong will. The following are a couple traditional ones:

Will Exercise 1: Single-Minded

Pick an object to look at. Candle flames, the second hand on a clock, or just a point on the wall will do. Simpler objects are often the best. Make a commitment to simply gaze at the object for fifteen minutes every day, at the same time of day, for one month. Then at your appointed time, set a timer for fifteen minutes, sit down, make yourself comfortable, and begin gazing. The goal is to focus entirely on the object. Do not let your eyes wander. Do not keep checking the clock. Do not let your mind wander. If any thoughts pop into your head, dismiss them and bring your focus back to the object. You will probably find that you will have to do this many, many times but do not let frustration distract you. Just bring your attention back to the object. Keep this up until your fifteen minutes are done.

Will Exercise 2: Word Play

Pick a common word in your everyday speech. You might pick "the," "and," or pronouns such as "he," "she," "you," "we," or "it." Any word that you use all the time is good. Now commit to not using that word for the next thirty days. Whenever you speak, be conscious of the words coming out of your mouth so that you do not accidentally say the word. If you do, punish yourself in some way. Make yourself do twenty push-ups or skip dessert every time you say the word. Keep this up even if after the first day it looks like you'll have to do a thousand push-ups and skip dessert for a year and a half. This exercise accomplishes two things simultaneously. First, it trains your ability to concentrate and be aware. Second, it helps you learn to discipline yourself and build willpower. At about three days into the exercise, you are going to want to stop or skip it "just today." If you can muster your willpower and push through, you will have come a long way in your magickal training. As the sneaker advertisement says, "Just do it."

However, as any realist will tell you, sometimes willpower isn't enough. Sometimes the obstacles are so large that brute power and perseverance just won't overcome them. That is why we also have a skillful will.

Skillful will is the application of that focused, committed drive toward finding a creative solution around the problem. So often we are like those movie characters who, in the rush to get through a door, keep trying to break it down until someone comes and tries the doorknob. All through school and life we are trained to fit in, to do things like everyone else, to stay in line. For that reason, many people's creative faculties atrophy. Therefore, to truly devote our will toward our desire, we need to adapt and try other methods of getting the outcome.

Will Exercise 3: Creative Viewing

Pick something disgusting to look at. It could be a full Dumpster, pet droppings, rancid meat, or whatever grosses you out. Now spend fifteen minutes trying to see it in a different way. Imagine that it is a piece of modern art and you are an art critic. What would you have to say about the artist's use of color, contrast, and shadow? How would you look at it differently if you were a photographer? What about if you were a starving person? How would a bird or insect see it?

Now pick something you find very attractive, such as a flower, or a person, or a place. Spend fifteen minutes trying to see it differently. If it is a place, how would a land developer look at it? A dog? A child? An elderly person? A disabled person? If your thing is a person, how would a surgeon look at him or her? A paranoid person? An axe murderer? How does he or she look to a head louse or mosquito? How would Picasso paint him or her?

Will Exercise 4: Creative Problem Solving

For the next several days, try to find one alternative, outrageous solution to every problem, large or small, that comes up. Make your solutions as fun and creative as possible.

Will Exercise 5: Creative Communication

Most people ask and say things without thinking about them and often don't listen for your answer because they expect them to be rote. When they ask "how are you today?" many seldom listen because most people routinely respond "fine." So for several days, commit to not giving rote or usual responses to people. When people ask mundane questions like "how are you today?" try to come up

*with creative answers they aren't expecting like "tall." Every time
someone asks you an either or question such as "are you going out
or staying home?" answer "yes." See how people respond. Likewise,
try to come up with alternative greetings yourself. Instead of "how
are you?" notice something about them and mention it. For example,
"Is that coat as warm and comfortable as it looks?" The process will
make you break out of mindless routines, allow you to notice things,
and help make genuine communication with people.*

The Higher Will is the Divine plan of forces that the Gods
have set in motion. You cannot go against their will for long.
Thus, it is better to try to understand the Higher Will and align
your will with it. In some ways, it is a bit like being a vegetable
farmer. By understanding the Divine plan of weather and pest
patterns in your area, you can plan your gardening accordingly.
You would plant water-loving plants during the rainy season,
heat-loving plants at midsummer, and frost-hardy ones in the fall.
If you fail to align your Higher Will with the Divine plan, you
will find that things are much harder. Your rain-loving plants will
die in the hot, dry season unless you take extraordinary mea-
sures, and even then you might not save them. Magickally, you
might want to do spellwork for finding your one true love. If that
is in accord with the Divine plan and both you and that person
are at the stage where it could work, then the Divine might let it
manifest. However, if it is not the right time, no matter how much
magick you do, it will not work. As an adept it is important to be
able to read the signs and work your magick accordingly. In a
later chapter, we will explore ways to develop your intuition and
connect with Divine inspiration so that you can better align to
the Higher Will.

To Dare: Imagination and Visualization

A creative, powerfully focused will that is aligned with the will
of the Gods and the forces of nature is a tremendous magickal

tool. But it is of limited value unless it has a clear target on which to focus.

Magick is the process of raising energy and directing it toward some particular goal. Imagination is the means through which you focus on your particular goal. Therefore, it is very important to develop your ability to imagine things and to be clear about what you imagine when doing magick. If your intention is vague, your possible outcome has more variables. It is kind of like just deciding that you want to go "somewhere" and setting out. Without a specific destination in mind, you'll end up somewhere but it might not be some place that you want to be. It is always much easier and more effective getting to your destination when you know precisely where you are going, have mapped out the best route, and have planned for all contingencies and alternate routes. So it is with magick. Imagination is the determination of precisely where to go, the skillful will is the planned route, and the strong will is the focus of energy to actually go. Most spell-workings or magick require that at least one person present has as clear and realistic a visualization/imagining as possible of the desired outcome—sensing every small detail, smell, sound, taste, and other nuances. The more detailed and realistic the imaging is, the more precisely the magickal will can be focused.

Imagination also fuels the desire to make manifest your goal. By imagining your heart's desire in as much detail as possible, you increase your desire, commitment, and will to make it so. In turn, your will ensures that you will focus your imagination and visualization on the prize. Like so much else in magickal practice, will and imagination create a mutually feeding and supporting feedback loop that spirals to higher levels of energy and focus. For example, the more I imagine all the details of what kind of perfect mate I want, the more I pine and desire it. That desire fires up my will to do everything in my power to bring that person into my life. As my will seeks ways to make my desire come true, it skillfully uses my imagination to come up with creative ways to attract him or her. My will also keeps me focused constantly on holding the image of my desire in my awareness, so that every action I do can be assessed as to its impact on my goal. Thus, my will and imagination feed and support one another and make my magick more effective.

The "dare" part of imagination is that for anything to become manifest, it first must be dreamed up by someone. But it takes courage to dream and hope. Many of the world's greatest inventors were called crazy for dreaming of things not yet real. But it was their daring to dream, and to then put their wills into finding a way to manifest the dream, that eventually made it true.

As for developing one's abilities, almost everyone has the ability to visualize and imagine to some extent. Most people can picture things in their minds, although there are some who cannot. Things such as tastes, smells, and physical sensations are typically harder for most people, but simply require more practice. Since the efficacy of one's magickal workings and meditations is often highly related to one's ability to visualize and imagine, it behooves everyone to become as skilled as possible. The following exercise is designed to build these skills.

Daring Exercise: Visualization and Imagination

Pick out a simple object such as an apple, a basketball, a candle flame, or anything else that you have handy. Try picturing the object in your mind and seeing every little detail from the color down to the texture of the object. How does it feel in your imagination? Can you smell it? If it is edible, what does it taste like? Does it make a noise? Is it hot or cold? Try to see, feel, smell, hear, and taste everything about this object just as if it were real. If you have trouble, get out the item and examine it closely. Then try again.

Keep doing this exercise with everything you can find, getting increasingly complex. Can you realistically imagine every detail about your dog or a friend? How about a whole place? Everything in the room and going on outside it? Can you imagine things moving and changing and not just in still life? With practice you'll get better. If you have particular trouble with even simple objects, try just seeing a color. Then try to see a colored dot, then a line, then a geometric shape, and so on.

If in the end you find that you are one of those people who just cannot visualize or cannot imagine smells or tastes, just focus on developing the aspects that you can do. Like a blind person with heightened senses of touch, sound, and smell, you will find that the aspects that you can imagine will more than compensate for those that you cannot.

In ritual work as well as in spell crafting, these skills in visualization and imagination should always be used. When you are creating a sacred space, it is important that you strongly imagine (using visualization, tactile sensation, smell, taste, etc.) the structures and symbols that you are creating. When you mark the boundary of the sacred space, it is important to actually "see" and "feel" the blue flame coming from your athame or finger and creating a flaming bubble around the circle. If you purify and consecrate the area, you should see the water and smoke wash away all negativity and invite in all that is sacred and positive. If in your tradition you trace magick symbols at the four directions while creating sacred space, actually see them hanging in the air where you trace them. For example, some traditions trace Water and Fire triangles at each of the four directions while they are purifying and consecrating the circle. Because water purifies, they draw a blue triangle with the point down symbolizing water at each direction. Another person then comes around and immediately on top of where the Water triangle was drawn, draws a Fire triangle. A Fire triangle is a red triangle with the point up and represents the divine power of fire consecrating the ritual area. When drawing these two triangles, it is important that you see them hanging in the air, so that when the red Fire triangle is traced over the blue Water one, they make a perfect hexagram symbolizing the union of the two major forces in nature — Fire and Water. You can always tell when someone isn't or cannot effectively imagine and/or isn't seeing the energy because he or she will trace the triangles crooked or not touching. The same thing applies if you trace the pentagrams in your ritual space casting. You should actually be able to see them, hear the blue flames crackling, and feel the heat of them around the circle protecting it from all unwanted influences. The ability to do this is what adds the magickal energy to the ritual and makes it other than simply pretty ritual theater. It is a distinction that many beginners miss.

As a practical matter, it is important when you visualize your desire that you make sure to include all the critical details but that you leave enough room for it to manifest in a number of ways. For example, if I want to get a book published, I should visualize holding the finished product in my hands. I should feel the weight and the smoothness of the pages. I should be able to smell the fresh ink and see the print font used. But I should *not* limit my spell by imagining it being published only by one publisher or it having only one particular set of cover art. My goal is to have a book published. The method of meeting that goal should be left up to the Divine. If I get too specific about noncritical items, I can make my goal incompatible with the Higher Will and thus impossible. Always be specific on the outcome, but not on the method of attaining the outcome.

To Know: Magickal Faith

So you have something that you desire. You have used divination and intuition to make sure that your desire is part of the Higher Will and can happen. You have been developing your strong and skillful wills and your imagination. You have used your imagination to stir up strong emotions and focus your will. You have a simple ritual all planned out and are ready to do it. This is where faith comes in.

Faith is the certainty that when you do a spell or ritual it will work. Faith is knowing that when you say "So mote it be" you are not lying to yourself or others. It is the certainty that you *can* make things happen using your magick. If you do not have that certainty before going into the ritual, then you will unconsciously put some of your doubts into the ritual and thus leave room for it to fail. So it is important that you develop your faith in your magick *before* you actually do it.

The way to develop faith in your ability is to make certain that you know that what you say is always true. Once you have learned that you always speak the truth, then when you say that something must be so in ritual, that must be true too.

Knowing Exercise: Truth-Telling

From this day forward, commit to never saying anything that you know is untrue or that might become untrue. This is more than not just telling lies or exaggerating. If you cannot know for certain that something will be true, then do not say it will be. For example, do not say "I'll see you on Tuesday" unless you are absolutely positive that your car won't break down or you won't get hit by a bus before then. If you cannot guarantee that you'll be there, then you should modify your statement to "I'm planning on seeing you on Tuesday." That is not to say that you won't make honest mistakes occasionally. Facts change. Remember when Saturn was the only planet with rings? Now we know that Jupiter, Saturn, Uranus, and Neptune all have rings. The important thing is your intention around what you say; that your intention is to always say only the truth.

Once you have spent several months where everything you say is true or will come true, then you will develop faith in your words. You know that if you say it will happen, that it will. That faith will then add power to your ritual rather than steal from it. However, if you are in the habit of small white lies and other untruths, then why should something happen just because you do a ritual and say that it will. You say lots of things that don't happen. This is nothing different. You have no faith in your words. Faith has power.

Furthermore, once you have done your ritual, your faith will keep you from worrying and wondering about the outcome of your ritual. One of the big mistakes that beginning spell crafters make is that after they finish the ritual, they keep thinking and worrying about it. They might even worry themselves enough that they repeat the ritual one or more times "just to be sure." The problem is that by thinking and worrying about the spell, they have not let go of it. Their minds, wills, and energies are still attached to it. If they are still attached to it, then it has not really been released into the universe to manifest. They have not created a ball of energy and intent to throw out into the universe and make things happen. They have created a yo-yo that keeps coming back to them and never makes it to where it needs to go. These rituals almost always fail, which further injures the person's faith in his or her own power. Therefore, it is critical to develop your faith. Remember, "A witch always keeps his or her word."

To Keep Silent: The Darkness

Seeds germinate in darkness. The unborn fetus grows for nine months in the darkness of the womb. The old Celtic calendar began each new day at sundown and the new year at the beginning of Winter. Silence and darkness are necessary for all new beginnings, and so it is with magick.

After a ritual or spellworking has been done, do not immediately talk about it. Many groups have prohibitions on talking about a ritual, any insights, visions, or anything that comes from a ritual until at least a day or two afterward. Talking about it diffuses the energy. It is like planting a seed and then digging it right back up. And with spells, talking about it afterward is another sign of not letting go of the spell. So make certain that you do not talk about your magick right away if ever. There is great power in secrets. Learn to keep them.

Furthermore, if you only ever say things that are true, and you learn to keep silent more than you talk, you will find that the power of your words grows both within yourself and within your community. We all know people who do not talk much but when they do, it is wise, important, and powerful. Be one of those people.

Raising Magickal Energy

The generation or "raising" of magickal energy is one of the primary activities of Wiccans. Magickal energy is used to create sacred space, heal, do spellwork, create, deepen spiritual awareness, induce trance, and a variety of other uses. Before we talk about how to raise and use this energy, perhaps we should identify what it is and how it can change.

"Energy" is defined as all the manifesting, vital, activating force in the universe. Everything in the universe exists because of the energy it creates and maintains as reality. A thing without energy manifesting it is just a collection of subatomic particles. Similarly, anything that is alive and/or moving and changing has an additional amount of energy. Thus, everything is and has energy, and all "types" of energy are variations of the same underlying energy. Therefore, when we say "magickal energy," "healing energy," or "solar energy" we are really talking about the same energy. However, due to the circumstances in which it is involved and what it is doing at the time, it appears to be and act differently. It is like waves on the ocean. All the waves, regardless of differences in size, shape, or direction they are moving, are part of the same ocean.

So if we use the energy we gather from the sun, we call it solar energy and because of its circumstances and location (as light and heat coming from the sun), it has particular qualities such as warming and illuminating that can be used in healing. Conversely, we can use the energy of water for cooling and cleaning. If we use energy from any source for magick, it is called magickal energy. But ultimately behind the various apparent qualities, all energy is the same.

Energy can be raised through a variety of methods and drawn from a number of sources. The manner in which the energy is raised and the source it is drawn from will in turn affect the apparent qualities of the energy.

Methods

Some of the more common methods for raising energy are:

Drumming
Chanting
Breath work
Movement and dance
Sex

Because energy is a dynamic force that by its very nature likes to move, any activity that encourages movement—physically, emotionally, mentally, or psychically—will tend to raise energy. Each of these techniques, if done where it begins slowly and builds to a crescendo, serves to push the energy along faster and faster, thus raising the amount of it. As excitement rises, so does the energy.

Commonly, several of these methods will be combined. When drummers drum, the rhythmic movements synchronize with their breathing and contribute to pushing their energy into the ritual. Likewise, the chanters and dancers serve to add to and move the energy around, which becomes stronger as the dancing, drumming, and chanting get faster and faster. It is also not uncommon for energy raising to be done in waves. The energy is raised and then allowed to drop down a little. Then raised again, this time higher, and then allowed to drop. Each wave gets higher and stronger. The succession of waves builds the pressure behind the energy until it is at last released.

Sources of Magickal Energy

While the drumming, dancing, chanting, or other method is taking place, additional magickal energy can be drawn from a wide variety of sources. As mentioned earlier, the energy drawn from these various sources will each have corresponding qualities. Some of the more common sources are:

The Earth

Pick a spot where you can sit or stand directly on the ground. Close your eyes, relax, and ground and center. Feel the earth below you. Feel the pulsing rhythm of the deep underwater rivers, the blazing molten core, and the ever-shifting tectonic plates. Reach down to the earth, imagining your hands going deep into her soil. Breathe in and feel yourself sucking the energy of the earth up into your body. Breathe in again and feel more energy rush into your body. Feel yourself filled with the heavy, powerful, nurturing energy of the earth.

The earth is an obvious and common source of energy for magick working. The earth holds, sustains, and feeds us. The minerals from the soil make up our bones and bodies. When we die we return to the earth. The earth is almost always a readily available energy source.

Celestial Bodies

Pick a bright, sunny spot. Close your eyes, relax, and ground and center. Picture in your mind the sun, blazing hot on a bright summer day. Feel the heat of the sun warming your skin and awakening your mind. Raise your arms up to it and imagine yourself pulling the energy of the sun into your body, causing you to glow with a bright yellow light.

Energy can also be drawn from celestial bodies such as the sun, the moon, the planets, and the stars in the sky. The energy from each has its own unique qualities. As you've probably experienced, the sun's energy is very bright and fiery. It is stimulating like a bright sunny day. The moon's energy can be very quieting, cooling, and meditative. It is also very deep, emotional, and intuitive. By reading up on the various astrological associations of each, and experimenting with them yourself, you will get a good sense of what kind of energy might work best for each kind of ritual.

Oceans, Lakes, and Rivers

Pick a spot where you can sit or stand next to the body of water. You may even want to touch the water with your hand or foot. Close your eyes, relax, and ground and center. Picture the water next to you. Now feel the water inside your body—your sweat, tears, blood, and other fluids. Like calls to like. Call the power of the water to come to you. Imagine yourself pulling the energy of the water into your body. Feel yourself filling up with the cooling energy of the water.

Energy can be drawn from any natural phenomena. In the case of water, the qualities of the energy you bring in will be strongly influenced by the type of water body you draw it from. The ocean has a different feel than a deep, calm pond, a raging river, or a small babbling brook. Water is usually cooling, calming, and refreshing, but it can also be powerful, suffocating, and uncontrollable.

Air and Clouds

Close your eyes, relax, and ground and center. Imagine yourself floating on a cloud up in the sky. Feel the winds gently rocking your body and you float there, weightless. Now in your mind, call the winds to come and lend you their power. Feel the power of air, cloud, wind, and sky fill your being through your nose and mouth with every breath you take. Feel it pouring in through the pores in your skin. Feel the power of air.

Energy can be drawn from each of the four elements. It can also be drawn without being in direct contact with it. You can contact Water through your blood, Air through your breath, Fire through your metabolic heat, and the earth through your bones. Some elements, like Air, can be both energizing and scattering like little breezes blowing every which way.

Natural Landscape

Go to your favorite place in nature. Find a comfortable place to sit. Close your eyes, relax, and ground and center. Open your eyes again and pick one object in your setting. It can be a tree, a stone, a plant, or a waterfall. While gazing at the object, in your mind ask permission of the object to draw some of its energy. If you get a positive feeling, imagine your pores opening up and that the energy of the object begins to enter you. With each inhale, feel yourself being filled

by the energy, wisdom, and knowledge of that object. Feel your en-
tire body and aura filling up with the energy. When you are done,
thank the object for the energy.

Energy can be drawn from anything, especially natural objects. Being animists, it is always good to ask permission before
taking energy from something and to thank it afterward.

Gods and Spirits

Close your eyes, relax, and ground and center. In your mind's eye,
picture a God, Goddess, or other spirit that you may have an affinity
or relationship to. Picture him or her until he or she is lifelike to you.
Ask him or her to lend you some of his or her energy. If you get a
positive reaction, open yourself up and feel the energy pouring into
all of your centers—your feet, palms, genitals, belly, heart, throat,
third eye, and crown. You may actually see the Divine being directing
the energy to you or touching you on each spot. See and feel each
center light up with energy.

Gods and spirits are great sources of energy. Their energy can
be very powerful, which can be useful for major magickal workings such as healing the very ill, helping the land recover after
strip mining, and manifesting peace in the world. The potential
downside is that each deity has his or her own personality, which
will affect the energy, and thus you. Warrior gods can be very aggressive, which can make you aggressive as well if you work with
them. This is good if what you want to bring into yourself is more
self-assertiveness, but not if you are seeking a peaceful and con-
flict-free life. For example, you might invoke the Morrigan, the
Irish goddess of battle and strife, to give you courage and
strength as you go to court to stop clear cutting. She will probably grant you that energy. In return, however, you may find that

you tend to pick fights with everyone, including your friends and partner. Thus, your whole life becomes battle and strife. So always be very careful about what energies you bring into yourself.

The Universe

Close your eyes, relax, and ground and center. Imagine that you can see the underlying fabric of the universe—the structure on which all of reality is manifest—Albert Einstein's space-time continuum. You might see a giant grid or web of woven strands of light and energy. Picture the entire universe filled with this energy. Now open yourself up to it and let it flow into you through your centers. With each inhale, feel the energy being inhaled not just through your nose, but also through every cell of your body. Imagine yourself being a conduit or empty vessel through which this energy flows.

For people who are familiar with Reiki, which literally means "universal energy," the sensation of the previous meditation will seem familiar, even if the meditation does not. Reiki practitioners work precisely with this underlying grid of universal energy. There is an almost unlimited quantity of energy that is the background structure of the universe, even in places scientists categorize as voids. This energy is always present, regardless of what other object, entity, element, God, or other thing is also present. Unlike the energy of the planets or Gods, this energy is mostly neutral in character, although it does tend to be healing.

Ancestors

Close your eyes, relax, and ground and center. Picture in your mind your parents, or people representing your parents. Now picture people representing your four grandparents behind them. Now pic-

*ture their parents, and move back up your family tree through your
ancestors. See the huge collection of people who each contributed
in some way to your being in the world today. Notice the large collection of skills and knowledge that this body of people represents. Feel
the wisdom and energy of this collective group. Now bring that energy into your body. Feel the power of your ancestors pumping
through your veins and circulating throughout your body.*

A part of your ancestors are always with you—in your DNA,
your family history, and the very spark of life handed down to
you from your parents. Done properly with care and respect,
your ancestors will guide you, provide wisdom, lend energy, and
even intervene on your behalf when necessary to support you.
The more you develop a relationship with your beloved dead, the
stronger the link becomes and the more benefits you can gain.
For example, in many African diasporic communities, the ancestors do everything from help remove illness and bad luck to bring
wealth and prosperity. More important, they can be excellent
sources of wisdom, guidance, information, and magickal energy.
However, be aware that working with your ancestors becomes a
relationship where both parties are expected to contribute their
time and energy to their mutual benefit. The more you give, the
more you get—just like any other relationship. And if you expect
to get something without giving back equally, don't be surprised
if your ancestors get angry. Their "payback" can be very harsh.

One's Self

As a last resort, you can always draw energy from your own
body. Frequently, people will try to give some of their vitality to a
sick or injured loved one. However, because there are so many
other sources for energy, you should never have to do this except
in the direst circumstances where every last ounce of energy that

can be drawn from every possible source is necessary for a life or
death situation. To use your own energy for any other purpose
runs a number of risks. If it is done frequently and recklessly, you
can deplete your essence, which can never be replenished. Once
this happens, if you continue, it will slowly drain you, make you
imbalanced, and eventually lead to degenerative illness and death.

Breath and Movement

As mentioned previously, breath and movement are valuable
tools for bringing energy in from various sources, raising large
amounts of energy, and then moving it around within the ritual.
Let's look more closely at how each one functions and some of its
uses.

Breath

Breath and our body's energies are intimately connected. If we
don't have breath, we don't have energy, and thus we don't have
life. Energy follows the breath, which is why in martial arts and
the Oriental healing arts the movement of energy, either to cause
injury or to remove blockages and create healing, is all coordi-
nated with and directed by the breath. The same principles apply
to magickal workings.

Therefore, as with martial arts, it is important to breathe during any ritual movement. When you are projecting energy outward for such things as casting the boundary of the ritual space,
you should emphasize the out breath. When you are bringing energy inward, taking the ritual boundary back down, or calling in
energy from a particular source for example, you should emphasize the in breath. In a similar vein, whenever you are tracing
magickal symbols in the air, you will find that the process is more
energy filled if you coordinate it so that every upstroke is with an

in breath, every downstroke is with an out breath, and horizontal strokes are done with held breath.

Breath is also a good tool for raising energy. Energy raised through quick, staccato breaths will cause things to heat up, including the energy of the ritual. Energy raised through slow, long breaths will slow, calm, and cool the energy of the ritual.

Lastly, breath is an excellent way to coordinate the energies of a group of people. By breathing together at the same rate, they begin to coordinate their heart rhythms, their mental functions, and their magickal energies. You will find that as people breathe together they will start moving, thinking, and doing things in perfect synchronization. One way to start this process is to make sure that everyone, especially the group leader, breathes audibly while circle casting, raising energy, and doing other magickal operations. The other members will automatically and unconsciously start to coordinate their breathing to the leader's and each other, beginning the synchronization process.

Movement

In occult science, there is a common dictum that movement in a clockwise direction (deosil) increases energy, and counterclockwise (widdershins) decreases energy. This is because deosil is sunwise, thus invoking the Light and power of the sun and the natural world, while widdershins is just the opposite. So when you are casting a circle, it is typically done clockwise, and when you take it down, it is usually done counterclockwise. Furthermore, while in circle you should pay attention that every movement around the circle (e.g., to get from the right side of the altar to the left side) is done in a clockwise manner. So for our example, that would mean walking all the way around the circle rather than just making the short counterclockwise movement from right to left.

Fluid movements, like the energy of a circle, tend to be calming and inwardly focusing. Sharp punctuated movements tend to be more aggressive, stimulating, and direct awareness outward. In a similar fashion, slow purposeful movements also tend to be calming and inwardly focusing as opposed to fast movements that tend to be stimulating.

Furthermore, moving with a relaxed body will tend to be fluid and grounding. Moving while keeping your arm, leg, and abdomen muscles tight will raise a hot, forceful energy quickly.

So if your goal is to go into a deep, relaxed meditation, a slow, fluid dance or gentle rocking forward and backward would be preferable. And if your goal is to ground out any unwanted energies while in the meditation, that dance might be done widdershins. However, if you want to raise a forceful, assertive, and expansive type of energy, then a fast, jerky deosil dance with many movements in straight lines and right angles and forced staccato breathing would get the desired results.

Posture/Mudra

Form and function are intimately related. Form dictates the functions that a thing can perform, and ideally the function should help one to decide which form to use. For example, a bowl-shaped object would perform the function of holding water better than a flat-surfaced object. The form dictates the function. So if I have a function that I need filled, in this case holding water, that function should determine which form I choose to use. In this case, I would most likely choose a bowl instead of a flat board. That is not to say that you couldn't use a board if you wanted to or if it was the only object available. It just wouldn't necessarily be the most efficient tool for the job. This principle is very important in all areas of ritual planning. Some ritual forms, designs, and ritual spaces are better suited to particular uses than others. It is also important in ritual posture.

In ritual posture, there are postures that are active and projective and those that are passive and receptive. To point at something is active and projective. To reach toward something with arms outstretched is active. To hold your arms in a posture as if to catch or hold something is passive and receptive.

For example, in many traditions when they are casting the circle, the arms and fingers are outstretched. They are projecting their magickal will and energy to create the boundary. When the Quarters are called, the person doing the calling stands in the form of a pentagram, palms forward (there is an energy center in the middle of the palms), projecting him- or herself in the form of a pentagram to the Quarter and actively calling the energy of the Quarter (Earth, Air, Fire, or Water) to come into the circle. He or she does *not* stand in the receptive pose of elbows at the sides, hands raised to shoulder level with palms up. That pose, which comes from Catholic ritual, is done when the priest wants to call God into himself. Many Pagans have just taken up the practice by default without thinking about its purpose or function. But because this is a receptive pose, it focuses the energy into the person doing the invocation. The funnel shape of this pose gives its function away. But while this is the right pose for invoking a God or Goddess into oneself, one generally does *not* want to call a straight elemental force into oneself. It is a quick way to become unbalanced energetically. If you have been doing that pose every time you called Fire into the circle and wonder why you have a quick, fiery temper these days, or why everything has become so volatile in your life, now you know why.

While the person is calling the Quarter, often the rest of the coven is standing in the "Magician pose," so called because it is the pose of the character on the Magician card in the Rider Waite tarot deck. It is with your right hand pointing up and your left hand pointing down to symbolize the principle of "as above, so below," and to actively direct the energy from the outside (the elements—"above") into the ritual circle (here and now—"below").

Both hands usually have the pointer and middle fingers held

together and extended, along with the thumb. This is because of the elemental associations with the fingers on the hand. The thumb represents Earth because it is the largest, most substantial of our digits and, being opposable, is important in our being able to manipulate our environments and to feed ourselves. The forefinger is Air because it conveys the pinpointed accuracy of thought and the expression of ideas. The middle finger is Fire, which is easy to remember because few gestures denote anger, ire, or passion more than an upraised middle finger. The ring finger is Water and emotion, which is why we wear our wedding rings there. The pinkie is the least substantial digit and thus represents Spirit.

So when they do a magickal working and want to project their will (Fire), directed by their imagination (Air) so as to manifest into reality (Earth), they use the forefinger (Air), middle finger (Fire), and thumb (Earth).

Gazing Up or Down

Besides hand and arm position, the direction of gaze can also have an effect on ritual outcome. I cannot begin to tell how many times I have seen a priestess invoking or praying to the Earth Goddess, arms and hands held upward, head thrown back, gazing up into the night sky. My question is always, "If you are invoking the Earth Goddess, shouldn't your imploring gestures and gazes be directed down to the Earth instead of up to the sky?" Usually she has no answer—she just does it that way. But the answer is simply this: she holds that posture and gaze because it is what is familiar. Growing up in a Jewish or Christian faith, such people are used to seeing the priest address God in that manner. But Yahweh/Jehovah is a sky God who lives "up there" in heaven. So that posture is appropriate for him or any other sky Gods or Goddesses. But when working with Earth Gods and Goddesses, you will find that things work better if you direct your attention toward, instead of away from, the object of your prayers and invocations.

To become an adept, you should practice the basics every day. An adept is skilled. Therefore, it is important that you have these skills down before you move to the next station around the circle of knowledge. Hopefully, as an intermediate practitioner you found that you already knew most of it. Those things that you did not know can now be integrated into and enhance your spiritual practice.

You may have found that some of these basics were in contradiction to the tradition in which you were trained. If that is the case, by all means keep doing things as you learned. There is no one right way to do things. Your tradition and intuition should always trump what any author might say. However, people who are truly adept at their spiritual practice not only know what to do but also why they do something and why others might choose to do it differently.

CHAPTER 2

Through and Beyond the Circle: Creating Sacred Spaces

J ust as skill is a hallmark of adepthood, so also are knowledge and flexibility. As an intermediate practitioner, you almost certainly have knowledge and experience in creating sacred space of some sort. As an adept, it is necessary to take that knowledge and experience and move it to the next level. This next level is the knowledge of precisely how sacred spaces are created, how they influence the work done in them, alternative forms of ritual space, and why you would want to choose one form over another. The goal of this chapter is not to teach you how someone else creates ritual space, but to present you with the tools so that you can create your own unique and more powerful spaces that in turn will make your magickal workings truly astonishing in their power and effectiveness.

Pagan rituals are usually done in sacred space. Sacred space is a place that is purified from any negative emotions or other irrelevant energies and dedicated or consecrated to the purpose of meeting, communicating, and working with the Gods and the spiritual realms. Unlike many better-established religions, Wiccan groups often do not have entire buildings, or even rooms, dedicated as sacred spaces. Nor are such buildings necessarily desired. Wicca, by its definition as a nature-worshipping religion, often prefers to have its rituals and worship outdoors.

Therefore, Wiccans usually construct sacred spaces anew every time they meet. Most introductory books on Wicca teach that Pagan sacred space is a circle. However, an advanced practitioner knows that there are other options that need to be weighed based on what we will be doing in our sacred space, its location, and purpose. There are times when the sacred space may need to take some other geometric and energetic shape such as a cone, square, or triangle. There is a spectrum of types of sacred spaces with varying strengths, limitations, and potential uses. An adept Wiccan knows these types, how they affect the ritual, and has the flexibility to design and create the sacred space that is best for the work being done. Cookie-cutter ritual outlines are fine for beginners, but true mastery requires knowing the nuances and subtleties.

Functions of Sacred Space

There are three primary ritual functions of a sacred space. These functions are:

Consecratory/votive
Protective
Containing and focusing

Consecratory/Votive Function

This function marks out the space as a different place from the mundane world, a place where something special is going to happen. One important effect of consecrating a ritual space to spiritual practice and the Divine is that the process of doing so focuses the minds of those present on the intent of the ritual. It begins the process of putting everyone in the right state of mind, open to their intuition and the inspiration of the Divine.

There are instances when this function is more or less critical.

Outdoor rituals, especially those in places that aren't highly trafficked public parks, often do not need this function as much. As Pagans, we tend to see the natural world as inherently sacred. So why try to sacralize something that is already sacred? The same idea applies to dedicated ritual rooms that have been consecrated once and the ritual space permanently established. There is no reason to keep consecrating it every time. The magickal charge is already present. However, rituals done in living rooms and other multi-use locations, including city parks, probably do need to be created and consecrated each and every time so as to remove any residual energy that might have been left behind by anyone who was in the space earlier. Especially if the sacred space is then deconstructed at the end of every ritual. Lastly, the consecratory function may not be necessary if no actual magick is going to take place. If the "ritual" is a discussion group or party, then while having the space cleansed and consecrated may help make the space feel welcoming, consecration probably doesn't need to be a major focus of the ritual.

Protective Function

Another function that sacred spaces may serve is as a protective barrier. There are times in ritual workings when it is desirable to control any influences from either inside or outside the ritual space. Rituals where the participants are going to open themselves, emotionally, energetically, personally, and/or spiritually should be controlled. Examples of such rituals would include those where a person opens up emotionally to his or her coven so as to ritually work on some deep emotional trauma, or when a priest or priestess opens him- or herself up as a channel for possession by spirits, elemental forces, or Gods. Being that open and vulnerable is akin to being surgically opened. Once open, the environment around the patient needs to be carefully controlled to make sure that nothing unwanted like germs or other contaminants enters the body. In the case of magick, the "germs" are unwanted thoughts, emotions, intentions, or other energies that may pass by either randomly or intentionally. You wouldn't want to prepare for Divine possession and just before your chosen God enters have some other spirit cut in and possess you first, but such things do happen. A less extreme example would be for a person to be in a ritual space trying to heal from the emotional abuse she received from her husband while at the same time he is intentionally or unintentionally projecting angry thoughts at her for leaving him. However, there are times when protection is less of an issue. Meetings, study groups, parties, and entirely celebratory rituals do not need to be as highly protective.

Similarly, spellworking is often best done in a highly controlled ritual space. When you are trying to do a spell for a specific outcome, you are much more likely to get that desired outcome if you can limit the number of variables that can influence it. Since spells work primarily energetically, they are easily influenced by outside energetic forces. Some such influences are obvious. You wouldn't want to do a spell to bring peace and harmony into your life with a war film showing on the television, or a healing spell surrounded by toxic chemical smells. Smells, sounds, and images can all have effects on your thoughts and emotions. These in turn affect your intention and concentration and ultimately your spell's outcome. Less obvious influences are more energetic. Energy workers, including Eastern healers and Wiccans, know that thoughts and feelings can create an energetic "charge" that can stick to things. So if I have positive thoughts while holding a rock, my thoughts will leave a positive energetic charge on the rock which the next person who touches the rock will feel. Conversely, if I sit in your chair while seething with anger, the next time you sit there you may unwittingly pick up some of that anger and feel yourself becoming irritable for no apparent reason. So it is important that the spellwork be done in a sacred space that is both clean of any charges, positive or negative, left behind and secure from any new outside influences coming in. The last thing you want mixing into your love spell is the bad mood of the guy walking down the hallway outside.

Containing and Focusing Function

In spell casting, healing, and several other kinds of ritual work, the ability to raise and focus a large amount of magickal energy is needed. Thus, ritual spaces can be created in such a way so as no energy escapes until desired and the energy is focused onto one particular person or thing. The space, then, becomes a large container of energy that is raised. The energy is raised until it fills the ritual container and is then directed by a person or thing toward its stated goal. However, study groups and other meetings that don't raise energy won't need this function designed into the ritual space. And even celebratory rituals, which often can raise large amounts of energy, do not necessarily need to contain and focus the energy if it is not being raised for any other intent or purpose than to raise it.

Qualities of Ritual Spaces

There are several qualities that can and should vary in sacred spaces based on ritual needs:

Portability
Permeability
Permanence
Shape

Portability is how movable a sacred space is once it has been created. It all depends on what the sacred space is attached to. Sacred spaces can be attached to a specific geographic spot such as a grove in the forest or a room in your house. These spaces would not be particularly portable. However, there are times when you might want participants to be able to wander over a large area. For example, some ritual hunts involve participants covering acres of land. In cases like this, a sacred space that was attached to the participants could spread out as far and wide as they do. Similarly, a ritual with a long processional march might want to attach the sacred space to a central pole, ritual rug, or sacred artifact that would be carried along in the processional.

Permeability is how easily things can pass through the boundary of the sacred space. Permeability and protection are closely related. The boundary can be configured anywhere from being completely open so that anything can pass through it to being completely closed to all energetic influences, and everything in between. Generally, the less permeable a barrier is, the more protection it affords. Alternatively, the permeability can be modified to serve more as a screen than as a barrier. That is, the barrier can be designed to be selective of what energies it lets in and out instead of just blocking all energy flow across it. Thus, I might create a boundary that is specifically designed to allow in love, happiness, and peace but not anger or aggression. Or I might create one that will only allow a particular God, Goddess, or other spiritual entity to pass but not all.

Permanence involves how enduring the sacred space will be. As discussed earlier, this quality can affect how necessary it is to consecrate a space. However, it isn't just as simple as a permanent space, once consecrated, never needs it done again while an impermanent always does. A permanent space, outside in nature, may not need consecrating at all. Nor may a room that is dedicated to magickal study and discussion but in which no energy is raised. However, you might rotate each month at whose house your coven meets. In this case, you might permanently consecrate a portable item such as a ritual rug or canopy that you could use anywhere anytime without much preparation. Some people call these "instacircles."

The shape of a container influences how people and energy

move within that container. This in turn affects the qualities that
the energy takes on and how it can best be used. Although there
is an infinite number of shapes that a sacred space could take, in
Wiccan and Pagan practice, the most common shapes are:

Circles/bubbles
Cones
Squares and cubes
Triangles
Lemniscates
Odd and amorphous shapes

Circles/Bubbles

*Close your eyes and take a moment to relax and breathe. Picture
in your mind that you are a particle of energy moving slowly in a
straight line. You have no will or desire to move in any particular way.
You are just a mindless energy particle. Imagine your particle self inside of a two-dimensional circle. As you move along, you eventually
find yourself moving parallel to the side of the circle. Notice how the
wall of the circle keeps corralling you around and around—always
folding you back inward toward the middle. Now imagine that instead
of a two-dimensional circle, you are entirely encased in a bubble.
Feel how this enhances the sense of inward folding energy. Like a
wave of water inside a glass globe, you swirl around. As the swirling
becomes more vigorous, you rise up higher and higher along the
side of the bubble until you suddenly roll over and crash back into
the center. What if more particles are added and spun faster and
faster? How does this feel to you?*

Wiccan circles are almost always bubbles. Because of the folding inward nature of the circular shape, energy in a ritual circle
also tends to keep focusing inward toward the center. Also like a

mixing bowl, the energy keeps mixing and meshing, reaching higher levels of integration. Therefore, circles are ideal environments for inwardly focused deep personal transformation work. They are also particularly good for creating the feeling of warm, cozy safety necessary for such work. Lastly, when energy is added and raised, the circles become like particle accelerators, spinning the energy faster and faster, the folding in quality just adding more energy to the process. This spinning and folding effect compounds and mixes the energy within and is why circles are good energy-raising shapes. Therefore, circles and bubbles are best for healing, personal growth work, charging magickal items, and other rituals where the energy raised will stay and be used within the circle.

Cones

Close your eyes and imagine that you are that energy particle again. This time you find yourself in a cone-shaped container. Notice how this shape is also circular but that as you go around, you find yourself spiraling upward into the cone tip. As you move farther into the tip, the circle circumference gets smaller and thus, each rotation get faster. How would this feel if there were other particles coming after you? What would happen when you got to the tip of the cone and the others came in behind you?

Cones have qualities similar to those of circles. They also fold the energy inward, raising and intensifying it. However, cones also tend to focus the energy more and pack it tighter, like grains of sand in the bottom of a paper cone. The more sand added to the top, the greater the focus and pressure in the cone tip. And if you keep adding sand, eventually the pressure will get such that the tip will burst and the sand will spray with pressure in whatever direction the tip was pointed. This same effect happens with magickal energy, which is why most spellwork is done in cones. A cone is created the same way as a ritual circle, however, this time the intention and imagination of the caster hold the image of the space being cone shaped. Spell energy is raised and pushed up into the tip of the cone. When the energy level is high enough, the cone tip is directed through will and imagination toward the targeted outcome and released. The cone shape naturally assists in this process.

Squares and Cubes

Close your eyes and imagine that you are that energy particle again. This time you find yourself in a cubic container. Notice what happens when you bounce off of one of the flat walls. Do you find yourself bouncing back and forth in a straight line? What happens when you add energy? Do you feel yourself bouncing more vigorously at a rapid rate? What if you are redirected toward another direction by a mirror? Do you find yourself ricocheting around the cube, your path forming one or another geometric shape? How does this bouncing between poles feel?

As you may have noticed, squares and cubes cause energy to move almost like a laser beam. By moving the energy back and forth between poles, it makes it stronger, more agitated, and more narrowly focused with each pass. When the energy is eventually released, it shoots to its intended destination in a highly charged and highly refined form. Squares are good for rituals about harmonizing polarities. A ritual where you wanted to balance out your impulsiveness with more forethought and discipline would be excellent for a square or cube. If you ever find yourself saying "on the one hand . . . but on the other hand," then you have two forces that can be harmonized by work in a square. Also, because of their laser effect, energy in squares is refined and narrowed rather than mixed into a collective as in circles. Because the goal of ceremonial magick is to attain enlightenment and unity with the transcendent God force by refining one's thoughts, emotions, and actions so as to attune oneself to the Divine Will, most ceremonial magick is done in squares. The square shape assists one in moderating extremes in one's life by balancing the opposing parts of one's personalities and focusing one's attention strongly and narrowly—like a laser beam—on the mind of God.

However, while a cone-shaped ritual space does focus and direct, it lacks the balancing effect and the heightened refining effect of a square or cube. Circles mix and increase energy, focusing it inward toward the center. Cones mix and increase the energy while directing it to some outward destination. Squares and cubes balance and refine opposing energies, increase the energy level, and focus the energy outward to a very precise destination. Wiccans who want to do balancing work or rituals around disciplining the mind and body may want to make occasional use of squares.

Triangles

Close your eyes and imagine that you are that energy particle again. This time you find yourself in a triangular container. Notice what happens when you move from the flat side toward one of the angles of the triangle—how you become increasingly focused and refined as the width of the triangle narrows. Also be aware of how a triangle, without the circular component that a cone has, directs the energy. Without the spirally effect as you move toward the angle, how does it feel different from a cone? Can you feel how a triangle has the focusing and refining qualities of a square and the directing qualities of a cone?

Triangles are traditionally used in ceremonial magick to invoke spirits from the other side. Similarly, some Norse magickal groups will use the triangle as a bridge from this world to the realm of the Gods. Because of the flat sides of the triangle, energy tends to bounce from side to point similar to a square, giving the triangle focusing and refining qualities, as opposed to the blending qualities of a circle. Additionally, because of the pointed angles of the triangle, it has the directing qualities of a cone. Thus, triangles are very good for reaching across and opening doors to other worlds. Circles fold energy back into the circle and are good for integrating and connecting the spirits and energies of this world together. Triangles, because of the outward directionality of their angles, are about creating links between two separate places.

Lemniscates

Close your eyes and imagine that you are that energy particle again. Imagine that you are in a large figure eight–shaped chamber. As you wind back and forth around each loop, passing through the center, notice how that feels. Does it feel like you accelerate around the loops and then slow as you pass through the center? Can you feel a charge building up in the one place that you always cross in the middle? What if there are more particles in there with you? What happens when several of you reach the center at the same time?

The lemniscate—the figure eight on its side—is a symbol of infinity. Like a Mobius strip, it is never ending. It represents the harmonious and balanced interplay between the conscious and the subconscious, ideas and emotions, positive and negative.

A ritual space created in the lemniscate has a particular effect. By working at the intersection point, the ritual participants are purposely putting themselves at the nexus point where they will be intensively bombarded by various energies. Lemniscates work best for magickal workings where the goal is to magickally imbue an item or person with some particular magickal energies. The focusing of energy on the single central spot will make the imbuing process very concentrated and intensely powerful. However, because the lemniscate's shape is balanced between two poles and brings the energy in from two opposite directions, they will tend to be balanced and thus reduce the chance that the person or thing will become unbalanced from the intensity of the process.

Odd and Amorphous Shapes

This is the practical form of creating sacred space. Beginners often learn that to do magickal work, they need to cast a circle. This can cause some distress and confusion when their available space is a long, narrow room or is L or T shaped. Fortunately, because magick is strongly influenced by intention, ritual space can be created in any shape. Granted, those shapes won't have the form-influenced qualities of circles, cones, squares, or triangles, but when reality dictates a different shape then that is what you have to go with. As Wiccan Elder Penny Novack says, "Reality always wins." It is probably better to have a sacred space, especially if you need the protective, consecratory, or energy containing functions, than not to have one at all. But remember, the shape you use *will* have an impact. The best way to get an idea of how the energy will flow is to do the meditation of you as the energy particle while in the room. Notice how you feel, what way you flow, and where you encounter obstacles or blockages.

Deciding on the Appropriate Sacred Space

When preparing to do ritual, the adept practitioner will take all the functions and qualities of ritual spaces into consideration. Beginners just do the ritual they were taught or read in a book. Adept practitioners, having given thought to the functions and qualities that contribute to a ritual's effectiveness, will custom design the sacred space to maximize the ritual's effect.

To decide on the appropriate ritual space, you have to decide which functions and qualities fit together in a way that matches the limitations of your physical space and the energetic needs of your ritual. There are particular functions and qualities that naturally fit together. Bubbles and squares are the most stable and protective shapes, but they wouldn't fit well together because of how they affect the movement of energy. Triangles, by their nature of being gateways, are less protective, but would be all right inside a square or circle. So if I want to do a ritual in my living room, a ritual that involves invoking my patron God, where I will do a specific spell casting and release the energy to the world, then I will want a ritual space that is consecratory because my living room is probably not always sacred, that is strongly protective to keep out unwanted influences on my spell, but that is specifically designed to filter out all energies except my patron God and is cone shaped for its containing and focusing qualities.

However, if I want to do a ritual (1) outdoors, (2) a ritual that is celebratory, (3) where we will be walking in procession from the trees to the lake, (4) and people wandering in and out, then I probably do not need the space to be particularly protective or focusing. I might simply attach the ritual space to the participants, making the shape amorphous as people move around. The boundary would be maximally permeable.

Or lastly, to use an extreme, if I wanted to do a ritual that (1) invokes something I do not want to physically or psychically connect with such as a physical manifestation of my fear or anger or an Otherworldly spirit with a tendency to bring chaos or harm, a ritual that (2) requires maximum protection and focus, then I might do as the medieval magicians did and create two ritual spaces. The first would be a very protective, nonpermeable, highly focusing ritual bubble in which I would sit or stand. Outside of that bubble, I would create an invocatory triangle inside of another protective circle. In this case, the triangle would be designed to invoke the being into the other circle. That circle would be designed as a barrier to keep what I invoked from getting *out* of the circle—essentially a box or prison in which to hold what is invoked. The protective circle around myself would be designed to keep the being or other influences from getting into my circle. That would keep unwanted influences from contaminating my ritual during the invocation, and after the invocation, would protect me in case what I invoked escaped its circle.

I would like to emphasize that there are huge ethical and spiritual issues around doing this kind of invocatory working. It is generally considered inappropriate to use magick to influence or control another being against his or her will, and to do so may have an adverse affect on your own spiritual development.. Do not attempt this kind of working without major guidance and assistance from someone knowledgeable and experienced in it, if ever. This is only an example to show how different ritual barriers can be constructed and combined.

Creating the Sacred Space

Now that the general concepts have been covered, and you have decided on the type of sacred space needed, all that is left to do is create the sacred space. The actual mechanics of casting are not too complicated. There are usually five steps in creating ritual spaces of any sort:

1. Grounding and centering
2. Marking of the boundary
3. Purification and consecration
4. Direction calling
5. Invocation of Deity

After the invocation of Deity, the actual magickal work is done. It can be simply celebratory, deep magickal workings, ritual enactment, spellcrafting, journeying, studying and practicing, healing, or some other kind of activity. This is usually followed by the sharing of food and drink, and then the ritual space is taken down. Unless you have been working with particularly baneful entities or energies, there is usually no need to purify or consecrate when taking down a ritual space. Therefore, there are four steps in removing ritual spaces:

1. Thank and bid farewell to Deity
2. Banish the Directions
3. Uncast the ritual boundary
4. Ground and center

The main thing to remember is that ritual intent and imagination are the core to any magickal operation. As long as you hold the intent to create a particular type of ritual space and use your imagination to see it happening, it will happen.

Examples will be given for:

Formal circle casting
Square casting
Triangle casting
Eye-to-eye casting
Informal ritual space castings
Alternative castings

The descriptions in these examples are fairly detailed and include additional information as to how each component affects the magickal outcome. They are composites of several traditions and styles put together as teaching tools. Grounding and centering were covered in chapter 1, so I'll simply list them when they should be done and not go over them again here. There is, however, one additional topic that needs addressing before we get into the various examples: altar placement.

Altar Placement

In a sacred space, the number and placement of altars has many variables. Some traditions have altars in each compass direction plus the main altar. Other groups skip the directional altars and focus entirely on the main altar. Other groups do a combination of the two, with altars in each direction, but one of them also being the main altar. Where the main altar is located has an impact on the focus of energies in the ritual. Each compass direction has specific magickal associations and whichever direction the main altar is located in will determine the focus of the ritual.

In the magickal world, the two most common altar placements are the North and the East. Those groups who place their altars in the North and start their ritual space casting there tend to focus on Earth-type magickal workings. These groups and their rituals tend to revolve around nurturance, grounding, reclaiming the dark, empowerment of women, Goddess worship, and earth activism. Those groups who place their altars in the East and start their rituals there tend to focus more on Air workings such as learning, knowledge, wisdom, enlightenment, and spiritual growth. Just as the East marks the sunrise of solar light, so these groups tend to focus on the growth of spiritual Light in its practitioners. It is also not uncommon for groups to place the main altar in the center of the sacred space, showing that the focus of the group and their rituals is on the Divine center.

Formal Circle Casting

Most Wiccan rituals are done in circles. Different Wiccan and Pagan traditions have many styles of casting circles. Some groups go around the entire boundary of the circle once, performing every step simultaneously. Other groups mark the boundary from three to twelve or more times. Directions can be called in successive order of East, South, West, and North or any other combination including opposing directions such as North, South, East, and West. The options are almost endless. However, in general, most circle castings follow the five steps outlined earlier: grounding and centering, marking of the boundary, purification and consecration, direction calling, and invocation of Deity.

Grounding and Centering

As stated earlier, grounding and centering should be done before any magickal operation. Refer to chapter 1 for details.

Marking the Boundary

After grounding and centering, the next step is to create a boundary between your ritual space and the rest of the world. The importance of this step varies depending on what you will be doing in your circle, but if you are going to be doing any spellwork, journeying, or deep personal growth/opening work, then you will want a highly protective and strongly delineated circle so that you can control what kind of energy comes into or leaves your circle. A good parallel would be that of a scientist preparing to grow an experimental culture. The scientist would want to do such an experiment in a controlled environment so as to eliminate any unwanted influences or outcomes. The scientist would, therefore, prepare a petri dish for use. Your magickal ritual is your experiment. Your marked out circle is your controlled environment—your magickal petri dish, so to speak.

For marking the boundary, you should ideally use an athame or wand. In a pinch, your pointed finger or some other object will do. The idea is that something that points can be used to project energy, which is what you will be doing. In chapter 5, we'll explore the precise reasons why an athame or wand is best suited. For now, start by standing in the direction best suited to your magickal focus—East for learning and growth, South for creativity and passion, West for emotions and Otherworld work, and North for empowerment and connectivity—and take a few deep breaths to focus your mind and bring energy into your body. On the last inhalation, point your athame, wand, or finger to the place that will be the boundary of the circle. With your exhalation, focus your gaze firmly on that spot, which will be at the circle's boundary, and begin walking clockwise around the boundary.

Because you are projecting your magickal will and energy into creating this boundary and energy follows the breath, you will be exhaling while you are walking around the circle and stopping when you have to inhale. In moderate-sized circles, this works out to exhaling from East to South, stopping and inhaling in the South, then exhaling while moving to the West, stopping to inhale there, and so on. You should inhale, drawing energy up from the earth through the soles of your feet, and then project the energy out through the tip of your athame while slowly walking around and marking the perimeter of the circle. While casting, you should envision that a magickal blue flame is extending from the tip of your athame to the edge of the boundary being cast—cutting the space from the mundane world and creating the wall of a bubble of magickal energy around it.

While tracing the boundary, many people recite various conjurations. Feel free to recite one from a book, make up your own version, or cast the boundary in silence. What is important is your intention, imagination, and will.

Upon returning to the direction in which you began, bring your athame down, kiss the blade, and put the athame away either in your belt or on the altar. The boundary is now cast.

Purification and Consecration

Marking the boundary serves the purpose of creating a barrier and container. The boundary keeps all unwanted energies from coming into the space and possibly contaminating your spell-working. At the same time, the boundary serves as a container that will hold and focus the energy raised in the ritual until it is released for a specific purpose. However, creating the boundary does not remove any energies that were already present in the space beforehand. Nor does it influence what kinds of energies will be worked with in the ritual space. For those tasks, we need purification and consecration.

Purification is the process of removing any residual energies from the space within the boundary. It wipes the area clean so that any new energies invited in or created will not be tainted by any influences from before creating the ritual boundary. The process usually involves walking around the boundary of the ritual space holding—and sometimes sprinkling—a container of mixed salt and water. Salt, representing Earth, and water, representing itself, are used because they are the two passive elements. Just as the earth and bodies of water tend to receive, hold, and eventually break down things put on or in them, so the ritual salt and water are perfect for attracting unwanted energies to them, binding those energies, and then neutralizing them by bringing them to ground. This provides the effect of purifying anything that comes in contact with them—in our case, the ritual space. To use our scientific experiment analogy, purification is equivalent to the scientist sterilizing the petri dish to make certain that there are no lingering contaminants in it that might cause unwanted outcomes in his or her experiment.

The actual process of purification and consecration can be done in several ways. Purification can be done by ritually sweeping the area, smudging it with sage incense, making certain noises and sounds, and most commonly, by sprinkling salt and water. The following is a sample purification ritual in common usage:

At your altar, add three pinches of salt to a chalice filled with water. Over the cup, draw a Banishing Pentacle of Earth (a five pointed star with the point up, drawn in one movement starting at the lower left-hand point and moving toward the top point, then down the right side and continuing on until coming back to where you started, then drawing a circle around it). The banishing pentacle is used to purify the salt and water so that they can remove unwanted energies from the sacred space. We use the sign of a pentacle (with a circle around it) instead of a pentagram (without the circle around it) because the circle binds the symbol in place. It is used on "things" where you want the energy attached. Pentagrams are used to project energy "somewhere." That distinction is often overlooked but will be very important later.

Carry the chalice of salt water around the boundary of your circle sprinkling as you go. When you get to each direction, stop, dip your fingers in the chalice, and trace in the air a triangle with the point downward. This is the symbol of Water. When you trace it, you can do so starting at the bottom point and going to the other two points of the triangle in a clockwise manner or start at the upper left-hand point and go around clockwise to end at the bottom point. It doesn't really matter which as long as you are consistent. Ideally, you should draw the triangle about shoulder width at its widest point. Once you have gone all the way around the circle, say "I purify with Water" and you are done.

Consecration is the process of raising the vibration of a ritual space to one suitable to working with the Divine. It makes the space sacred. This is equivalent to the scientist adding a suitable growing medium to the petri dish and thus creating an environment conducive to growing what is desired. In our case, the process of consecration involves moving around the boundary with incense, preferably one in accord with the intent of the ritual that will follow. Incense is used because it is a combination of Fire, the flame of the incense, and Air, the smoke from the incense. In nature, fire and wind push things around, make things move, and generally stimulate activity. In the case of circle casting, it is a combination

of these two active elements that stirs up and raises the energy of
the ritual space. Therefore, purification should be done before consecration and not the other way around. Otherwise you'd be purifying, and thus undoing, the work you did when you consecrate
the space.

Consecration can be done through incenses that invoke various magickal influences, chants and instrumental tones, and ritual gestures. The following is the method commonly used with
the previous purification:

*At your altar, light a stick of incense. You may want to pick a par-
ticular scent that you know that your God or Goddess enjoys. Over
the incense, draw an Invoking Pentacle of Earth (a five-pointed star
with the point up, drawn in one movement starting at the top point
and moving toward the lower left-hand point, then up to the upper
right-hand point, across to the upper left, and around coming back to
where you started, then drawing a circle around it). The invoking
pentacle is used so that the fire and air of the incense will call the
Divine energies into your sacred space. Again, we used the pentacle
instead of the pentagram so as to bind the influence to the place.*

*Carry the incense around the boundary of your circle. When you
get to each direction, stop and with the incense stick, trace in the air
a triangle with the point upward. This is the symbol of Fire. When you
trace it, you can do so starting at the top point and going to the other
two points of the triangle in a clockwise manner or start at the lower
right-hand point and go around clockwise to end at the top point.
Again, the triangle should be about shoulder width at its widest point.
Ideally, you should also draw the fire triangle so that if you could see
them energetically, you would see the fire triangle overlapping the
water triangle to form a perfect hexagram—the symbol of the union
of Heaven and Earth, Fire and Water, God and Goddess. Once you
have gone all the way around the circle, say "I consecrate with Fire"
and you are done.*

Direction Calling

Calling the Directions is used to seal the circle. During the callings, the power of the four elements of Earth, Air, Fire, and Water is invoked to lend guidance, assist in the ritual workings, and protect the space from any unwanted influences. In the scientific experiment analogy, this would be equivalent to the scientist making any minor adjustments to the growing medium in the petri dish, perhaps adjusting the acidity level, and then sealing the dish to protect it from any outside germs or other influences.

The Direction callings are typically done one at a time again starting in whichever direction reflects your focus or intention. Various Wiccan traditions associate the directions with different elements. The most common association is: North/Earth; East/Air; South/Fire; West/Water; however, I know of at least one tradition that puts Water in the East and Air in the South.

As explained in chapter 1, the person doing the calling for any particular direction should stand in the pentagram position—legs shoulder width apart, arms extending directly outward to each side with palms facing forward. In this position, you are reflecting the pentagram of all four elements, plus Spirit at your head, in yourself. You are one with elements. And since this is a pentagram, as opposed to a pentacle, it is not tied to a place and thus can be used to project your will out to call and invite the elements back into the circle. While the caller is in the pentagram position, the rest of the group should stand in the Magician's pose with the right arm extended up, forefinger and middle finger at a place about level with the top of the person's head, and the left arm, fingers held similarly, pointing down to the earth. This posture is designed to assist in linking this earth-plane ritual space ("so below") with the Divine realm ("as above").

The caller should take a few deep breaths, send his or her consciousness deep into the earth, then with the inhale, bring the energy up to his or her heart and out to his or her arms—extending his or her arms as he or she feels the energy moving outward through them. The caller then should call to the Quarter, projecting an image of him- or herself in the pentagram position to the ends of the Universe. There are many variations of the invocation used for the quarters. Some are written in rhyme such as: "Fire burn, fire bright. Join us in our circle tonight." Others use simple prose such as: "Lords and Ladies of Fire, I summon, stir, and call you up to be present in my circle, assist my rites, and protect me from any unwanted influences coming from your direction." I have even seen very powerful silent callings. People use music, dance, and random vocalizations. All are fine as long as the will and intention are clear that what you are doing is projecting yourself out to invite the elements to enter the ritual space, assist the magickal workings that will take place, and seal and protect the space from any unwanted external influences.

After the invocation has been done, the caller often then traces the Invoking Pentagram of Earth as described earlier making sure to coordinate his or her breathing with each movement. Each upward stroke is an inhalation; each downward stroke is an exhalation and a held-breath during the horizontal movement. If working in a group, the others should do this along with the caller. At the end, the caller, and group if present, usually says, "So mote it be"—an old Freemasonic phrase meaning "so must it be." Then a candle is lit in that Quarter to symbolize the presence of that element. Each Quarter is invoked in turn, by different callers if possible, until all four compass directions have been called.

Invocation of Deity

The final step in creating ritual space is the invocation of Deity or whatever other kinds of spiritual energies you would like in your circle. People who see the Divine as immanent everywhere and thus not needing invoking, just invoke "center." However, people who work with a limited set of select deities will invoke those specifically. Other types of Pagans might invoke a list of God and Goddess aspects with various chants or invocations. Charlie Murphy's seven Goddess chant of "Isis, Astarte, Diana, Hecate, Demeter, Kali, Innana" and its related seven God chant of "Pan, Poseidon, Dionysus, Cernunnos, Mithras, Loki, Apollo" are popular pantheist invocatory chants. Others might prefer simply to say the God's or Goddess's name out loud, in a whisper, or silently in their minds. When speaking to your Gods, there is no right or wrong way. The important thing is that they be invited into your ritual space. However, I would recommend that you "invite" them but not expect or demand that they come unless it is critical to your ritual. No one likes to be ordered to attend an event and the Gods are no exception. Try to order them at your own peril. Furthermore, I'd like to reemphasize that unless it is your intention to draw a particular Deity into yourself, then when you invoke your Gods you should not do so in the palms up, receptive pose. In and of itself, the pose is probably not enough to make divine possession happen, but there is no sense in encouraging it either if you don't want or need it. At this point, your ritual space is cast.

After the ritual space has been completely created, the work of the practitioner or group can proceed. Refreshments usually follow the ritual work and then the ritual space is uncast.

Uncasting the Ritual Space

Once the ritual work is done, the ritual space must be taken down. The process is done in reverse order from the way in which it was cast, skipping the purification and consecration step. These steps are: thank and bid farewell to Deity, banish the Directions, uncasting the ritual boundary, and grounding and centering.

Farewell to Deity

As with invoking Deity, this can be as formally or informally as feels right. But it should involve bidding farewell to all the various deities and forces that were invoked. To invite them and not thank them and say good-bye would be impolite at best and depending on the deities involved, potentially dangerous.

Banishing the Directions

This process is done in the reverse of the invoking. You should start in the direction you ended at and move counterclockwise, bidding each Quarter farewell. Again, you might start in the Pentagram posture. Using a similar technique to the one you used to call the Quarter, thank it for being present, assisting you in your rite, and protecting your ritual space. As with the invocation, this is often followed by tracing a Banishing Pentagram of Earth as described earlier. Upon completion, it is common to bid the Quarter "hail and farewell" and extinguish the quarter candle.

Removing the Ritual Boundary

This is also done in the reverse manner from which it was marked. Again using your athame, wand, or pointed finger, start in the same Quarter in which you began and ended marking the boundary in the opening. Take a few deep breaths to focus your mind and then, after your last exhalation, bring the point of your athame up from the floor to a position just about level with the crown of your head. With your next inhalation, focus your gaze firmly on either the point of the athame or the spot that the athame is pointing to at the boundary of the ritual space and see and feel yourself sucking the energy back into your athame.

Because you are now withdrawing your will and energy from the boundary, most of the walking around the circle will be done while inhaling, stopping to exhale between movements. For example, in a moderate-sized circle cast beginning in the East, this would work out to inhaling from East to North, stopping to exhale in the North, then inhaling from North to West, stopping to exhale again in the West, and so on. After going all the way around the circle, you should point the athame to the floor, or ideally touching the athame to the floor, and exhale all of the drawn in energy down into the earth. While uncasting, you should be envisioning the magickal blue flame being sucked back from the edge of the ritual space into the athame and down through your body into the earth and the bubble of magickal energy being slowly erased.

The person uncasting usually ends with the words, "The circle is open and yet unbroken . . ." And is joined by the rest of the group, if any, in finishing with "merry meet, merry part, and merry meet again. So mote it be."

Grounding and Centering

After every magickal operation, all the participants should ground and center again. This serves to clear away any excess energetic charges that may still be lingering after the magick and to integrate and organize one's personal energies again. The ground and centering rituals mentioned earlier work very well for this purpose.

People who skip this step often feel giddy and light-headed, perhaps a little wired after ritual. After a powerful ritual, if you do not ground and center, you can expect to get the "post-ritual hangover," which feels very much like any other kind of hangover. It is definitely no fun. However, if you never ground after a ritual and don't get the hangover, then either you aren't letting any of the energy in or you aren't raising as much energy as you think you are. Both would be things to work on.

After grounding and centering, it is time to pick up the ritual tools, food dishes, and so on (if it isn't your ritual, always be a good guest), say good-bye, and head home.

Square Casting

Every thing about casting a square ritual space is the same as with the formal circle casting except marking the boundary. After grounding and centering, begin in the East with athame in hand and trace the square in a clockwise manner. Walk in a straight line visualizing the projection of blue energy from the tip of your athame forming an impenetrable barrier. When you get to the corner, make a sharp ninety-degree turn to the right and continue marking the southern boundary. Continue around each corner until you return to where you began in the East. Your square should be oriented so that each flat side is facing one of the four compass points.

Purify, consecrate, call the directions, and invoke Deity as in the formal circle casting. However, in moving around the ritual space, remember that it is a square. Therefore, whenever you walk around the ritual space, be sure to "square the corners," never walking in curves but instead always turning on your heel military-style.

After your ritual workings, you uncast as in the formal circle casting, except doing so in a square formation.

Triangle Casting

Remembering that triangles are best used to invoke beings from "the Otherworld," begin by ascertaining which direction would be best from which to invoke the Deity or spirit. For example, you might want to call a Water Goddess from the West and an Earth God from the North. Or you might want to choose the direction based on the God's or Goddess's specific myths. For example, if working with a Norse pantheon, you would probably want to invoke it all from the North, whereas the Celts tended to see the Otherworld as to the West. The important thing is that you make this decision consciously.

For this example, we will be invoking from the North. After ground-

ing and centering, face in the direction from which you will be invoking. Turn to your right, and place a lit candle or stone on the floor marking that corner of the triangle. In our example, that would be the southeast. In your imagination, trace a line from that corner to the corner in the southwest. Place another stone or lit candle there. Continue turning until you are back facing to the North. Take your third stone or candle and walk straight ahead to the North. Place the lit candle there and walk back to the South. Facing the North, imagine that you are projecting the candle farther and farther to the North, pushing it beyond the boundary between this world and the realm of the Gods. Once you can sense that the third corner is firmly set in the Otherworld, your ritual space is cast. You can now purify, consecrate, and invoke as usual.

When removing a triangle, after thanking and bidding farewell to the invoked beings, imagine the candle moving back across the boundary between the worlds and back into the room. When it is back, walk directly up to it, put out the flame, and bring the candle back to the center of the space. Pick up the other two corners in reverse order to how you laid them out.

Eye-to-Eye Casting

The priest or priestess starts the casting by turning to the person on his or her left. The priest or priestess makes eye contact with that person and says "eye to eye." Then taking the person's right hand in the priest's or priestess's left, he or she says "hand to hand." Lastly, touching their hands to his or her heart and then to the other person's heart, he or she says "heart to heart, I cast this circle." This should all be done slowly and deliberately. The person to the priest's or priestess's left then turns to the person on his or her left and repeats the process. The process continues around the circle until it comes back to the priest or priestess on his or her right.

Because this ritual space is attached specifically to the ritual participants, it is permeable and portable. People are now free to let go of each other's hands and wander around as the ritual allows without breaking the circle. What is holding the ritual space is the intent of the participants to be the ritual space. That is, by the participants holding the intention that they collectively comprise the sacred space wherever they go, then the ritual space follows suit. When people need to go home, they make a formal announcement that they are leaving to the rest of the people present and consciously break themselves from the circle. When a critical mass of people has left, the circle will dissipate without having to be formally uncast.

This ritual space is not particularly focusing, containing, or protecting, but it can be combined with a ritual purification and consecration, Quarter callings, and such.

Informal Ritual Space Castings

All the previous examples are formal, some more so than others. It is important that you know how to do formal castings in case you ever need them, but many times you won't. I listed them first because they are great examples of various techniques that can be done and what effect they have on the ritual space. The point to remember is that an advanced practitioner doesn't just repeat the exact ritual form he or she was originally taught. He or she knows what effects each component of the ritual has and caters each ritual space to the precise needs of the ritual.

In many cases, you won't need such a formal ritual. If you are doing a simple divination for yourself, you might want to simply close your eyes and picture a shimmering bubble of energy starting in your heart and expanding out to just a few feet around you. Picture all negativity draining out of the bottom of the bubble. Briefly go around in your mind and acknowledge the four directions and God and Goddess at the center of your bubble, which would be in your heart. Now you're ready to go.

Alternative Castings

There are many alternatives and combinations that can be made. You can create a containing, protective ritual cone, but then send individuals out of the cone by having them create personal bubbles around themselves and then stepping out of the circle through a temporary gate. Think of it as like sending an astronaut on a space walk. The circle is the protective spaceship and the personal bubble is his or her spacesuit. Or you might want everyone to do "eye to eye" before leaving the circle. However, you might want to start a quest ritual with "eye to eye" to create the ritual framework, and then have everyone go out to find various items for the construction of the formal circle. People might be instructed to go into the woods and find a feather for East, a rock for North, a stick for South, and water for West. They would then bring these back and these would be used for the formal circle casting.

Another alternative is to have everyone cast a ritual dome over the participants. The edges of it could be attached to a number of poles, candles, or stones that could all be picked up and carried from place to place. It would be an energetic canopy or blanket that could be processed. It would allow the ritual to move but still keep everyone in the same container. The possibilities are limited only by your imagination. As long as you keep in mind the general properties and qualities of energy, you can create a ritual space that truly is customized to the situation, intent, and needs of the ritual and its participants. Knowledge and flexibility are signs of magickal adepthood. By combining your knowledge and flexibility of creating sacred spaces with the energetic skills of chapter 1, you are now ready to take the next step around the circle of magickal knowledge: the world of advanced divination.

CHAPTER 3

Beyond the Crystal Ball: Advanced Divination

A depts are aware. They are alert to all the forces operating around and on them—celestial, terrestrial, societal, political, Divine, and archetypal. They are connected to the master plan of the universe—the will of the Divine—and thus they can choose how to live in harmony with those forces. A major tool that adepts use to ascertain these forces is divination.

Because tarot cards, runes, astrology charts, I Ching coins, and a host of other methods are easily available at almost any local bookstore, divination is one of the first skills learned by most beginning Wiccan practitioners. They usually start out by referring to books and memorizing the meanings of tarot cards, runes, or other tools. By the time they have the symbols and meanings of the tools not only memorized but also ingrained into their psyche, they have reached an intermediate level. Only when you have reached a point where you do not use tools at all, or if so only as gateways to intuition and clairvoyance, can you consider yourself adept at divination.

What Is Divination?

Divination is the process of "seeing" a whole situation, including the patterns and events that have led up to the present, the various influences and factors bearing on it, and, based on those patterns and influences, seeing how the future is likely to evolve if none of these are changed. In this regard, it does have a fortune-telling effect in that it is sometimes possible to predict what is likely to happen in the future. However, it is not so much seeing the future as it is seeing both the past and current situation clearly and extrapolating from them what the future might look like. It is important to remember, though, that the person receiving the reading is always in control and can, by making changes in his or her life, change the outcome of the reading. In fact, the real reason and value of divination is to see how one's life might come out and based on information from a reading, make the necessary corrections to create positive growth and change. A reading's outcome is never set in stone.

How Does Divination Work?

There are three main theories on how divination works, and in the end, they all come down to the same final conclusion. The first, synchronicity, says that there are no accidents or random events in the universe. Everything is part of the unified whole and aligned with everything else. Thus, the fall of cards, the turn of a rune, and the pattern a flight of birds make are all synchronized reflections of the greater pattern of the universe. The card that turns over in a tarot reading is the only card that can be turned at that particular time. It is preordained. Similarly, any event that happens to a person is also a reflection of the whole and thus any object or event can be used to read the pattern of life. The reader only needs to be open to seeing the patterns and how they fit together.

The second theory suggests that cards, runes, images in a mirror, and such are simply highly complex and ambiguous symbols or images that trigger the reader's intuition. The reader's psychic ability is what sees the greater patterns and provides the reading.

It doesn't really matter what image or symbol comes up; it is the focusing on the image that triggers the insight. The intuition of the reader executes the reading. The cards, runes, symbols, and images are vehicles that help the process happen.

A third approach combines the first two main theories. This integrated theory explains that due to synchronicity, the appropriate symbol or image will appear to trigger the insights and intuition of the reader so that he or she can see patterns correctly. The symbols or images that appear are not random but are themselves not sufficient to see the whole picture; they require a reader's intuition to reveal them. It is only from the intuitive state that arises from looking at those images and symbols that the insight comes.

The main common feature of these theories is the importance of intuition and/or clairvoyance. Intuition is the ability to know something without any apparent source of prior or current information. We receive and act on intuition almost daily though we often don't notice it. Advanced divination is fine-tuning your intuition and learning how to tap into it at will. Clairvoyance, sometimes called distant or remote viewing, is the ability to clearly see things far away without aid. While they are often talking in terms of linear feet or even miles, some clairvoyants include the distance of time as well. Thus, it is possible to actually see what happened in the distant past or will happen in the distant future.

What distinguishes an adept diviner from an intermediate one is the degree to which these abilities are developed. True adepts do not need to have any tools whatsoever. They can tap into intuition and see the greater pattern at will. They may prefer to use tools, as tools can give structure to a reading and provide an easy link to the person asking questions. They can also help the person being read feel involved in the process, which may, in turn, increase his or her investment in making necessary changes. However, the tools are not truly necessary.

Developing Intuition

There are a number of exercises that can help you develop these skills.

The basic format that you will see repeated throughout is:

1. Relax; ground and center.
2. Quiet the mind.
3. Open yourself to external and internal cues.

The best way to develop your psychic ability is to use it as often as possible. Therefore, the key to developing your intuition is to find many minor opportunities during the day to note your psychic impressions and then check to see how accurate they were. Some simple techniques for doing this are:

Intuition Exercise 1: Caller ID

Whenever the telephone rings, fight the immediate impulse to answer it or check the caller ID. Instead, take just a couple seconds to exhale, quiet your mind, and see if you can guess who is calling. Then check the caller ID or answer the phone and find out. You may surprise yourself at how often you are right. However, if you aren't right very often, don't worry. With time, you should find that your accuracy rate improves.

Intuition Exercise 2: The Next

While waiting in line or sitting in a waiting room, try to intuit what shirt color the next person who comes around the corner will be wearing. Or if you can see outdoors, what car color will drive by next? What song will come on the car radio? How many dogs will

you see on your drive to work today? How many women or men?
How many bicycles?

By practicing these exercises regularly, you will gradually improve your accuracy at predicting things. As your performance improves, your confidence will rise and you will be able to follow your hunches and impressions with much less worry. However, intuition does not have to be a passive process of waiting for inspiration. You can also actively pursue knowledge and guidance.

Intuition Exercise 3: Self-Guided Meditation

Find a quiet place where you can sit undisturbed for a while.
Close your eyes and take a few moments to breathe. Feel your
breath coming and going from your nostrils, causing your chest to
rise and fall. Quiet your mind and focus on your breath, relaxing any
parts of you that may feel tense. Once you are settled, picture your-
self sitting in a comfortable chair in the middle of a bright sunlit green
meadow. Notice the green grass, the wild flowers, and the buzz of in-
sects. Become aware of the blue sky with just the slightest wisps of
white clouds slowly moving across the sky. See the green and brown
of a forest in the distance. Smell the scent of the field and feel the
heat of the sun and the gentle caress of a light breeze on your
skin. Take in all the sights, sounds, scents, and sensations of the
meadow.

After fully experiencing the meadow, notice a dirt footpath leading
off into the distance toward the forest. Follow the path. As you walk,
feel the ground under your feet. Observe any animals, birds, or in-
sects. Again, take in the entire experience of the walk.

The path eventually comes to the edge of an ancient forest.
Notice how the smells have changed as well as the different bird
songs, the shift in the temperature of the air, and how the interplay of
light and shadow on the ground and in the trees is different. Follow
the path into the forest.

The path winds slowly through the forest, around ancient oaks, under the canopy of spreading maple and chestnut. The floor of the woods is spongy and very earthy. Under the canopy the ground is covered with occasional patches of fern. Take notice of the wildlife of the forest, perhaps spying a deer, a rabbit, or even a predator such as a wolf.

The walk eventually opens up into a small clearing in the woods. A beam of sunlight has penetrated the shadow of the canopy here and streams into the middle of the clearing. There, sitting on the stump of an old tree, is a person. From a distance, because of his or her position and clothing, it is impossible to tell whether it is a man or woman. Approach the wise elder of the woods.

Greet him or her and introduce yourself. The elder exposes his or her face to you, acknowledges you, and tells you his or her name. Take notice and remember this name. He or she then asks you what brings you into the forest. Tell the elder that you have come to seek information and guidance in a matter and that you would be most grateful for any help that can be given. Listen to what he or she tells you. He or she may also show you something or even take you somewhere. Allow the elder to guide you to what you need to know.

After the elder has finished, give thanks, and ask if there is anything that can be given in return. Listen to what is said and commit to providing it if at all possible. Ask the elder if you may come here again when you need guidance and take note of the answer. Finally, say thank you one more time and bid farewell. Leave the forest clearing. Follow the path you arrived on through the woods back to the edge of the meadow. Continue across the meadow back to your chair and sit back in it; picture yourself coming back into your body in this time and place. Once you feel like you have fully returned, open your eyes and write down your experiences. If you committed to giving or doing something for the elder, make a concrete plan now as to when and how you will meet this commitment and follow through with it.

You have now met one of your personal spirit guides. This being can be relied on to give you guidance whenever you need it in the future. Simply return to the forest glen and ask.

Developing Clairvoyance

In any situation, there are events and activities going on that are not readily apparent. Clairvoyance can be a valuable tool for seeing what factors may be in play that are contributing to a problem at hand. The purpose of the following exercises is to help you develop your skill at viewing anything at a distance. While we are using cards to begin with, once the skill is attained, it can be used to view any person, place, or event.

Clairvoyance Exercise 1:

Shuffle a deck of playing cards and place the deck in front of you with the cards facing down. The goal is to correctly guess the color of each card while it is still face down on top of the deck. As with intuition, the key to being successful in clairvoyance is to get your rational mind out of the way. Your first impression is the one most likely to be correct. Start by quickly looking at the top card of the deck and note what color you think the card is. Is it red or black? Turn the card over and see if you are right. Record your hits and misses on a sheet of paper. Do not judge yourself or become frustrated if you get something wrong. Conversely, do not get too excited about getting a card right. Either strong emotion will get your intellectual mind working and blur your subsequent seeing. Go through the entire deck in this way and then tally your total hits and misses. Statistically, if this is by pure chance, you should have gotten about twenty-six right and twenty-six wrong—50 percent. And in all likelihood, that is the total you will get. Don't be discouraged if you do worse than the statistic. Just keep repeating the process at least once a day for several weeks. Eventually, you will notice the number of correct guesses increasing or decreasing substantially. Either outcome is acceptable. If a real majority of card guesses are wrong, then you know that you are simply inverting what you see in a way similar to a photographic negative. So if you see red, call black and vice versa. Once you are consistently getting a success rate of 70 percent—thirty-seven out of fifty-two cards right—you can move on to the next step.

Clairvoyance Exercise 2

Having mastered distinguishing red and black cards, your can re-fine your skills by repeating the exercise but this time trying to see the suit of the card—clubs, spades, hearts, or diamonds. Chance guessing would yield thirteen correct guesses out of fifty-two, or 25 percent. See how much better you can do than that. Again, keep practicing for several weeks until you have a success rate of at least 70 percent.

Clairvoyance Exercise 3

This exercise moves beyond seeing objects into viewing places.

Find a quiet place where you can sit alone and undisturbed. Sit down and close your eyes. Take a few breaths to quiet your mind and relax your body. Once relaxed and quiet, try to picture what you would be seeing straight ahead of you if you opened your eyes. Try to notice every little detail—the play of light and shadow, textures, dirt and dust, everything. When you have the image clearly in your head, open your eyes and compare what you saw to what you really see.

The first time you do this, you will probably miss a number of things. That is all right, close your eyes and look again and see what is there. Then open your eyes and compare once more. Keep trying to see what is before you and then opening your eyes to compare until the image in your head perfectly matches reality. Over the next several weeks, try to do this exercise every day until you can get it perfect the first time. Once you've mastered that level, try seeing *what is behind you. As you master each step, keep expanding your range—try looking at the room next door, or if you will be visiting a new place, a room you have never seen yet. Once you have those mastered and can see them in your mind perfectly the first time you try, attempt to see what is going on downstairs or over at a friend's house. Then go to these places and check your accuracy. This skill can take a long time to develop, but once attained, it can be invaluable for a whole host of magickal purposes. Knowledge is power and seeing persons, places, and events from afar gives the adept a better understanding of the world around him or her. This understanding can then be used to create more effective spells, healings, and other magickal workings.*

Please be aware that not everyone has the same ability to visualize and see things in their minds. Many people are better with sound, smell, physical sensation, or emotional reaction. If you are not a visual person, try the previous exercises by using a different sense. How do you feel when you have a red card? Perhaps a slight smell comes to you for black? Or red cards make you itch or angry or you hear a faint high-pitched ring. Similarly, you may not be able to actually picture a person or place, but the person or place might elicit a particular emotion or body sensation in you. All are acceptable ways of perceiving objects hidden or at a distance. The challenge is to find how your particular cues correlate to actual reality. Once you know how to translate them, it is just as effective as "seeing."

Applying Intuition and Clairvoyance to Tools

At some point in our divination experience, we discover that it is acceptable to deviate from the strict meanings given by books or teachers and start to interpret the cards, runes, or other tools based on our feelings and intuitions. We realize that the tools are no longer literal answers to the questions, but instead have become triggers or channels to our intuition and clairvoyance. The depth and accuracy of our readings become tremendous. We are now using the tools as ways to connect to a higher source of information where both small details and the big picture can be seen.

Many years ago, I was doing a tarot reading for a young woman whom I'd never met before. She gave me no information. I cannot recall what the first card was that I turned, but looking at it triggered an image in my mind that the reading was about a young man, about six feet tall, with blond hair with whom she was having some kind of argument. When I mentioned what I saw, her mouth dropped open and she exclaimed that I was right. Her question was about her six-foot-tall, blond, blue-eyed boyfriend with whom she'd had a fight. The insights into her life were equally detailed and cut so quickly to the issue at hand that both she and I, as the reader, were left dazzled and stunned. Times like those are when you know that you really are connected to a higher source of information.

The following is an exploration of how your intuition and clairvoyance can be applied to some of the more common divinatory tools. Even if you use different systems than those presented, these examples should give some idea of ways that intuition and clairvoyance can be used to deepen and improve your readings. Because this is a book for advanced practitioners, the assumption is that you already have at least a basic familiarity and proficiency with some of these tools. Therefore, I won't be defining or explaining any of the basic methods or interpretations for these systems. If you do not know one of them, you should either focus only on the ones you do know, or go back, pick up an introductory text on divination, and learn the system before proceeding further. You have to know the basic general system (e.g., various card layouts, basic rune meanings, etc.) before you can move onto advanced work.

Tools: Tarot

With tarot readings, the most common approach is to lay out a number of cards into a particular configuration where each position represents some aspect of the questioner's life. A card that falls into a particular position in a reading is giving information about that aspect of the person's question. For example, a card that falls into the environment position of a layout would give insight into the context in which the question is arising. For example, is the environment supportive or hostile to the person and his or her desired outcome? What are some of the complications caused by outside factors?

Beginning readers will simply repeat what the books say about the card and try to interpret that in light of the position. However, there are ways to use a particular card to trigger your intuition and clairvoyance and thus get much more information for the reading. These exercises will help develop the ability to use each card as a trigger.

Tarot Exercise 1

Begin by formulating a question in your mind. Draw a card at random from the deck. Turn the card over and look at the picture on it. At first, do not try to remember what you may have read about the meaning of the card and its various symbols. Just look at the card and note if your eye is drawn to any particular part of the card. Many times, a particular image on the card will jump out or you will notice something on the card that you hadn't before. Once that image has drawn your attention, focus specifically on it and ask yourself how that image, either independently or as part of the larger whole of the card, speaks to the question. If it is at a specific position in a reading, ask how that image also relates to that position. For example, if the card that comes up in the environment position is the Fool and the image that jumps out is the small dog nipping at his heels, ask your-self what insights this image provides into the environment sur-rounding your question. Repeat the process for the rest of the spread.

Tarot Exercise 2

Think of a question you would like answered. Draw a card at ran-dom from the deck. If there is a person, creature, or thing in the pic-ture that you could imagine communicating with in some manner, ask that being "what are you here to tell me?" and then imagine it an-swering your question. For example, in the Moon card I could imag-ine myself asking the dog and coyote, the lobster, or even the face in the moon to tell what it means. Do not judge as to whether this is just your imagination or not, it doesn't really matter as long as you have developed your intuition in the previous exercises. Your imagination will be your intuition talking. Listen to what the image has to say and then interpret that into the rest of the reading. Even if you have not completed the exercises, if you go with your first impression, it is still likely to be correct. We use intuition unconsciously all the time. An adept knows how to do so consciously as well.

Tarot Exercise 3

Think of a situation where you would like more information or in-sight. Draw a card at random from the deck and hold it in your hands. Look at the card and take in the general impression of the card. Does it seem to provide good or bad news? Are there any sugges-tions or insights that immediately come to you? Next, while gazing at the card, try to imagine it being a door. Imagine the card splitting down the middle like double doors and opening up. Once the doors have swung open, notice any images, ideas, feelings, or thoughts

that were behind the doors. These are intuitions clarifying or ex-
panding on the general meaning of the card. Note these insights and
include them in your interpretation of the reading. This technique is
most useful when you draw a card for a reading and standard inter-
pretations of the card are vague or do not seem to fit the rest of the
reading.

Tarot Exercise 4

While holding a question in your mind, draw a card at random
from the deck and look at it. As in the previous exercise, imagine the
card opening up like double doors. Inside the card, imagine encoun-
tering a person, animal, plant, spirit, or otherwise. Ask the being to
give you insight into the meaning of the card and pay attention to what
it tells you. Give thanks, imagine the door closing, and add this infor-
mation to your interpretation of the card.

Tools: Runes

There are several methods of rune reading. Unlike tarot cards, runes tend to be simple images. Each rune, however, can have a fairly wide scope of interpretations. Fehu, for example, can mean fulfillment of ambitions, nourishment from the Divine, profit and wealth, and conservation of resources. As in tarot, some rune readings include laying the runes out into particular formations where specific positions refer to specific aspects of the question or person's life. The advantage of the simplicity of the rune im-ages combined with the wide scope of interpretations is that it naturally encourages the use of intuition. These exercises can also be used to make the intuitive link between the rune image and its specific interpretation for a particular reading.

Rune Exercise 1

Formulate a question in your mind. Draw a rune at random and look intently at it, noticing each line, angle, and curve. Then, in your imagination, either with eyes open or closed, let the lines of the rune glyph extend. See the rune expanding into a picture or image. It may resemble the original rune design or it may become something very different. Perhaps the image even expands into a storyboard telling a story. Use these new images as ways to inform and expand your interpretation of the rune in this particular reading. For example, the image of Berkana as a primitive B, which usually indicates some kind of actual or symbolic fertility, might extend into an image of a pregnant woman giving me insight that the fertility of this card is not symbolic at all this time. Time to paint the baby's room!

Rune Exercise 2

Pick a topic that you would like insight into. Draw a rune at random. Take note of which rune you draw and then close your eyes. In your imagination see the giant World Tree—its roots digging deep into the underworld, its branches reaching up into the heavens. Bound and hanging upside down from the branches of tree is the Norse god Odin, blood streaming from the place where one of his eyes once was. At the base of the tree is the rune that you drew. Odin speaks to you, telling you the meaning of this rune for this reading. This may or may not agree with what any of the books say. Nonetheless, thank him for his assistance. Open your eyes and consider how his words apply to your topic.

Tools: Astrological Charts

Astrological chart interpretation is both a science and an art. Although computers have greatly simplified chart casting, there

is still a substantial body of information of what the various planets, houses, and aspects mean that needs to be known to interpret
a chart in anything but the most superficial manner. Anyone who
has ever printed out an online chart interpretation has certainly
noticed that many parts of the reading directly contradict other
parts. The art comes in getting a feel for a chart and knowing
how to weigh the various aspects and influences. The many times
that I have had highly skilled and knowledgeable astrologers interpret my birth or natal chart, I have noticed that each astrologer
focused on a different aspect. The big picture was always the same,
but each picked up on different aspects that were also highly sig-
nificant. My feeling is that they were tuning into their intuition,
which was telling them what was most relevant for me to know at
present — even from a natal chart.

As with the tarot and rune exercises, these astrological exercises assume that you truly are an intermediate astrologer and
have basic knowledge and skills in chart creation and interpretation. If you have this skill level, these exercises will provide you
with additional tools in which to gain insight into a chart reading.
If you do not have the skill, you should either skip this section or
go back and learn the basics from some other book or class before proceeding.

Astrology Exercise 1

*If you do not already prepare them as such, cast the chart with
the angles of aspects drawn out on a piece of paper. Before examination and interpretation, take a moment to get the feel or gestalt of
the chart. Gaze at it without looking for specific aspects, houses, or
influences. Just take in any general patterns or shapes formed by
the lines of the aspects. Do you see squares, triangles, or other geometric shapes above and beyond the ones that you would expect?
Allow your imagination to see pictures and images in the aspect*

lines. What do you see? Do they give you any particular thoughts or feelings about this chart? Look at it again. Do any particular configurations or aspects catch your eye or jump out at you? Take note of them. Finally, interpret the chart as usual, but take into consideration what you've seen and felt—your intuition is guiding you.

Astrology Exercise 2

As a chart interpreter, you occasionally find situations where two or more aspects create a complex, often contradictory, reading. In these situations, note which planets are involved. Close your eyes, relax, and ground and center. Picture one being for each of the planets. You may want to choose the God for whom the planet is named, or some other being—Mercury or Odin for Mercury, for example. Once you can clearly see them in your mind's eye, greet the beings and introduce yourself. Ask them to explain to you their meanings and their relationship in this reading. Pay close attention to what they tell you and any other thoughts, images, or ideas that may come to mind. Otherworldly beings do not always speak in words, but often send images, emotions, or thoughts directly. When they have finished, thank them for their assistance. Open your eyes and continue your chart reading. Hopefully, the dialogue between these beings will give you previously unknown insights into the dynamics of reading and thus a more accurate interpretation.

Tools: Scrying

Scrying is the gathering of images, thoughts, feelings, and impressions by gazing at or into an object such as crystal balls, mirrors, still pools or ponds of water, candle flames, and bonfires. It takes some practice to scry because there are no limitations on what images might arise and no guideposts as in runes or tarot cards. Thus, it is up to your intuition to tell you what these images mean. Your intuition picks out the image that will come to you and then provides the clues on how to interpret it. This makes scrying one of the most advanced divinatory tools, which many people find difficult to master.

Scrying Exercise 1

Select the item that you are going to gaze into. A dark mirror (a piece of glass painted black on the back side) is good for beginning scrying. Crystal balls, water in a dish (often with a dark dye added), flames, even tea leaves in a cup will work. Take a few moments to relax and ground and center. Holding your question in your mind, close your eyes and clear your mind of any hopes or expectations of what you might see. Once your mind is clear, open your eyes. The trick is to look at the mirror or other item with "diverted attention." That is, you don't want to look directly at the item; you want to focus your gaze about six inches to the side of it so that you see it through your peripheral vision. The mirror should still be in your field of vision, but you won't be focused on it. As you gaze, you will eventually notice images beginning to arise. They will most likely form and then dissolve. As each arises, you can treat it as you did the tarot and rune images: Ask what they are trying to tell you or open them like a door to give you clarification. Take note of what you learn while resisting the temptation to look directly at them because as soon as you do, they will be gone. Continue to gaze until you feel that you have seen everything there is. You may see one image that arises and stays, or you may see a sequence of images as in a movie. More commonly, a series of seemingly unrelated images will become apparent. However, if you are successful in speaking with some of the images, a better sense of how they all fit together will be gained. Scrying takes time and practice to master. If you get a mish-mash of images and have trouble sorting through what they all mean, do not get discouraged. You can now do a tarot or rune reading to get further clarification on what you saw while scrying. For example, if I got a series of seem-ingly unrelated images such as a cat, an umbrella, and the state of Utah, I might simply ask the tarot for one or more cards that would help me understand the connection. Then I could pull a card and using the skills learned earlier in this section see what insights it pro-vides.

Divination Without Tools

Divinatory tools can provide easy and fairly accessible triggers to your intuition. However, like all things, they have their limita-tions. The most obvious limitation is that they require cards, runes, or other tools to be present when you do the divination. Another limitation of working with divinatory tools is that your outcome can be influenced and/or limited by the symbol system of the tool. Each tool is created based on some cultural, philo-sophical, and/or religious assumptions about how the universe works. By learning and using a particular system and its symbol set, you are at least temporarily looking through the lens of that system. For example, the tarot is based on the Jewish mystical sys-tem of the Qabalah. That system makes certain assumptions about how the universe works, what is culturally acceptable, and so on. For that reason, on a very superficial level, it is rare to find a tarot deck with same-sex couples and why the Ten of Pentacles shows an ideal family of two opposite sex parents, two children, and an elder, which hardly matches the reality of many modern Pagans.

On a deeper level, the tarot assumes a universe built of polari-ties that need to be reconciled, evidenced by the several cards with the black-and-white pillars, the polarity of the Lovers, the black-and-white sphinxes of the Chariot, and numerous other cards. In contrast, the I Ching is based on a Confucian doctrine that does not include such polarities but instead presents a sys-tem of proper interaction and relationship in all social, personal, and religious contexts that was believed to reflect the divine order. By observing these relational conventions, one's proper conduct brought him or her closer into harmony with the universe.

Thus, by using any system you are operating within the assumptions of that system and your readings will be colored by those assumptions. This is not necessarily a problem if you are aware and either choose your tools to match the intention and needs of the person being read for, or modify what you see to be more inclusive of options outside of the system. For a person who does not believe in duality or polarity, the I Ching might be a better choice than the tarot. However if the tarot is all you have, at the least trying to find possible nondualistic meanings in the cards might help.

The apparent solution to the problem of a system's inherent cultural bias is to divine with no tools whatsoever. However, don't be fooled into thinking that you will escape cultural bias. Each of us was raised and lives in a particular culture. Many Pagans have made a point of questioning our culture's assumptions, exploring a variety of alternative and subcultures, and adopting the parts that work for them individually. Nonetheless, we are still strongly influenced by the consensus reality of the mainstream in which we were raised and still live, sometimes known as the "overculture." As a privileged white, middle-class male, there are aspects of life as an inner-city black woman that I cannot understand and I would be arrogant to think I can. I have no context for it. So we should avoid thinking we can ever do divination without bringing our own biases to it. At best, we can meditate, get therapy, and do as much introspection as possible to minimize our most glaring biases.

Doing divination without tools is really an extension of scrying. Instead of scrying with man-made tools or artificially creating a setting for the scrying such as lighting a fire, we scry with what is at hand. I divide the arbitrary division of toolless divination into three categories: natural phenomenon, liminal spaces, and spirit readings.

Natural Phenomena

You can scry anytime, anywhere, with anything. You can use the pattern in the wood grain of a table, the reflection in a windshield, your screensaver, your dog's coat, a mud puddle—anything. Of course, being Pagans, we have a particular affinity with nature, which provides such a variety of beautiful opportunities for scrying.

Scrying in Nature Exercise 1: Flight of Birds

Formulate a question in your mind. Go outside to a place where there are flocks of birds. They can be starlings near an old barn, snow geese in autumn, a murder of crows sitting on a telephone wire, or any other collection of birds. Take a few moments to relax, ground and center, and clear your mind. Once your mind is clear, open your eyes and watch the birds fly using "diverted attention." Take note of any symbols or images they draw or other thoughts or impressions that arise. What does your intuition tell you about how they relate to your question or situation? Continue gazing until you have the feeling that you have seen everything there is to see.

Scrying in Nature Exercise 2: Clouds

Come up with a question that you would like answered. Go outside on a day of mixed sun and clouds at a place where you have a clear view of the sky. Close your eyes and perform your usual grounding and centering and clearing your mind. When you are ready, open your eyes and scry the clouds as they float by and take different shapes. Pay attention to any shapes, symbols, or images they form or other thoughts or impressions that arise. Try to figure out how they relate to your question or situation. Keep scrying the clouds until you feel like it is enough.

Scrying in Nature Exercise 3: Fire and Smoke

Go outside and make a small fire. Alternatively, burn some incense or start a small, safe fire in a fireplace or similar place. Holding your question in your mind, close your eyes, relax, and ground and center. Drop any thoughts or expectations of what you may see. As you open your eyes, scry into the fire and smoke. Notice any images or shapes in the coals, flames, or rising swirls of smoke. When you feel like you have seen what you need to see, spend some time considering how it relates to your question.

Scrying in Nature Exercise 4: Wind

With a question in mind, go outside on a windy day. Look for a place where you can see how the wind swirls the long grass or shimmers through the leaves of the trees. After your usual preparations of relaxing and clearing your mind, open your eyes and watch the patterns and forms that the wind makes in the grass or leaves. Note any shapes, symbols, or images that form or other thoughts or impressions that arise. What does your intuition tell you about how they relate to your question or situation? Continue to gaze until you feel that you have seen everything there.

Liminal Spaces

Liminal spaces, or "thin spots" as a friend refers to them, are places that are between other places or that straddle two or more spaces. Examples would be the threshold between two rooms, the line where the driveway and the road meet, half in and half out of the shadow of a tree, or on the stairs between floors. Times and dates can also be liminal. Dawn and twilight have always been considered magickal times precisely because they are between day and night. Similarly, Pagan holidays such as Samhain and Beltane hold particular power because they are between the seasons of Summer and Winter. Liminal spaces are particularly magickal because they are "between the worlds" and thus are places where the veil between this world and the world of magick is thin. Hence the name "thin spots."

Liminal spaces can be used for divination because information from the Otherworld can more easily pass over into your awareness. Thus, a liminal space will only heighten your intuitive abilities. The more thresholds you can combine, the more liminal and powerful the space is. Thus, if at twilight on Samhain eve, you can stand with one leg on the staircase and one in the threshold between the stairs and the room above, all the better!

Liminal Spaces Exercise

Find a thin spot outdoors somewhere. Standing in the liminal space, close your eyes and formulate the question in your mind. Once the question is strongly in your thoughts, begin to slowly rotate in place. Keep rotating until your intuition tells you to stop. Upon stopping, check with your intuition as to the direction that you should be looking. It will tell you to face upward or downward, to the left or right, or any such combination. Open your eyes. The first object, person, or place that you glimpse is your sign. Take note of it and ask your intuition how this relates to your question or situation. If you don't get an easy answer, try the techniques of picturing the item in your mind and having it open as a door, or ask it to speak to you and tell you what it means. Reflect on how to apply this information to the question at hand.

Spirit Readings

Spirit readings are the final level of advanced divinatory practices. They do not utilize any of the aids to direct intuition. No
tools, places, situations, or even external senses such as vision are
used to trigger insight. Instead, the adept makes a connection
with the person in his or her mind and then psychically opens up
for any and all insights that come.

Spirit readings can be done for a variety of reasons. On the
most superficial level, they can be used to do readings to answer
questions for people just like with runes, card readings, and astrology. In fact, this is precisely what legitimate psychic readers
are doing when they just look at you or talk to you on the telephone and give detailed readings.

Spirit Reading Exercise 1: People

*First, relax and ground and center. Establish in your mind some kind
of link to the person for whom you are reading. If that person is present
or you have a photograph, look briefly, then picture the person in your
mind. If you are reading by telephone, listen to the voice and get an
image in your head. You can even get an image of someone from
e-mail or letters. Don't worry if it is not physically accurate, the image
you have is the person's essence, which is what is relevant here. Once
you have a picture of the person in your mind, close your eyes and
clear your mind of any thoughts, preconceptions, or outside distractions. When your mind is clear, allow it to open up and accept any images, impressions, thoughts, or other pieces of knowledge that come
to you. If the person is present, either in person or by telephone, share
these impressions and get his or her reaction or feedback. Allow that
feedback to settle, clear your mind again, and see what arises again.
Continue this process until your intuition tells you that you are done.
Help the person being read to find ways to use the new information in a*

positive and constructive manner. For example, if in a reading you pick up that a person feels trapped in an abusive relationship, try to help with finding ways out of it. Or if the insight is that a person is about to lose his or her job, help the person understand that this advance warning is beneficial and that it is advantageous to start looking for new career opportunities earlier rather than later.

More deeply, spirit readings can be used periodically throughout the day to guide you into living and acting in ways that will create harmony, balance, and happiness in your life. By checking in periodically to see how your decisions and the decisions of others around you are affecting your life, you have the opportunity to continually adjust your life choices so as to create the maximum amount of fulfillment. It is precisely due to this skill that magickal adepts seem to never actually cast spells. By using their intuition, they can keep their lives attuned to the natural flow of the universe—living in harmony and balance. People only need to do spells when they have fallen out of harmony and need to correct something they have done or failed to do. If you have worked your way through the previous stages of divination, then this last step should be simple in concept.

Spirit Reading Exercise 2: General

Begin with your usual relaxation and grounding exercises. When your mind is clear, with your physical eyes either open or closed, simply allow whatever intuitions arise to come into your awareness. They may be visual images, thoughts, feelings, impressions, or even just a "knowing" about a thing or situation. They should come quickly and clearly. Continue to receive them until your intuition tells you that you are finished. Use these insights for positive, constructive growth in your life.

If your mind is wandering along with any images or thoughts that you have, then you are daydreaming, which is distinctly different from intuition. That is the primary danger of not having a tool or image on which to focus. But with some practice you should be able to tell the difference. You know that you are in the zone with spirit readings when the information comes quickly and effortlessly while still remaining focused and aware.

Ethics

No discussion of divination would be complete without a discussion about the ethics involved. There are four major points:

1. Just because you *can* know something about someone doesn't mean that you *should* know it without his or her consent. Don't be nosey.

2. Once you know something about someone, you have a responsibility to only use that information to his or her benefit, or to not use it at all. It is unethical to take insider information and use it to your own benefit. This is why point number one is important. If you make a point of eavesdropping on people, you will eventually know enough about people so that it will be hard not to use the information. However, if you use it without their consent, regardless of how well intentioned, you are violating their free will. Every person has the right to make his or her own decisions about how his or her life will go. If you presume to know what is right for another person without checking with him or her, and then try to impose your ideas without his or her consent, you are violating that right. And while not all Wiccans adhere to the Wiccan Rede, which states that it is all right to do what you want as long as it harms no one or violates anyone else's free will, or the Threefold Law, that whatever you do comes back to you three times,

most would agree that to use the information without consent would be unethical.

3. Even the best diviners are not 100 percent correct 100 percent of the time. Everyone has off days, so always take your findings with a grain of salt and get outside verification whenever possible.

4. Reality always wins. Spectral evidence, including intuition and clairvoyance, is always suspect. Just because something comes from the Otherworld or through psychic means does not guarantee that it is correct, proper, ethical, or right. You may see something as true, but if reality appears to contradict it, reality is probably right.

If you have been doing the exercises in this chapter, you are now adept at divination. By developing your intuitive and clairvoyant abilities, you have become aware of the subtle cues that the universe gives as how to live magickally. An adept can use the tools of divination but does not need to. This has given you a major tool in creating the change that will help you attain the masterpiece of your life. The next step to adepthood is to become not only aware but actually attuned with the forces of nature and the will of the Gods.

CHAPTER 4

Sun, Moon, and Stars: Deepening the Wheel of the Year

An adept is attuned. Having developed the ability to divine the general forces and influences in his or her life, the next task in the circle of knowledge is to attune to the ebb and flow of nature and the cycles of the Gods. In the previous chapters, I alluded to connecting and harmonizing with the Divine will. In Wicca, a major tool for making these connections is the Wiccan ritual calendar known as the Wheel of the Year.

As an intermediate practitioner, you are already aware that the ritual calendar is comprised of eight sabbats and thirteen full moons. In your reading and trainings, you've probably been exposed to some of the major mythic themes used by various groups. As an adept, it is necessary for you to have knowledge of several such themes. They can then be combined and overlapped to obtain deeper insight into the flow of nature and its reflection in our lives. These insights will aid you in this next step of ascertaining and attuning to Divine will.

Please note that all the dates given for holy days are approximate. Some events, like equinoxes and solstices, vary by a few days every year. Similarly, there are traditions that calculate their holidays astrologically rather than calendrically. Thus, their dates may vary by up to a week from those listed.

The Common Wiccan Calendar

Close your eyes. Picture in your mind a giant, eight-spoked wheel lying on its side. Where the spokes meet the rim of the wheel, there is a scene taking place. On the northern end of this wheel, where the spoke meets the wheel rim, it is a dark, cold Winter night. All is calm and quiet. The people and animals are bundled in their beds and sheds. The fires are burning low in the hearths.

On the opposite side of the wheel, where the spoke meets the southernmost part of the wheel, it is a bright, hot, sunny day. The trees and grass are leaved out and the flowers are blossoming. The livestock are gently grazing while the people are out planting, tending their herbs and vegetables, and enjoying the day. A clear running brook runs nearby where the children and dogs cool themselves with yells, yaps, and giggles.

At the eastern spoke end, it is Spring. The grass has begun to grow and the planting season has begun. At the western spoke end, it is Fall and the harvest is under full swing as are preparations for the long Winter to come.

In the northeast, between Winter and Spring, the scene is of a barn just before sunrise. Inside the barn, by the light of a single candle, the ewes, heavy with milk, are beginning to give birth to lambs.

In the southeast, between Spring and Summer, there is a maypole dance taking place. People, young and old, are dressed in spring flowers and bright ribbons. Many have bells tied about their ankles as they dance. Flirtation is everywhere and there is love and passion in the air.

In the southwest, between Summer and Fall, a great country fair is happening. Farmers from all over have brought their goods and families to the fair. They are trading goods, catching up on news, and holding competitions of skill, strength, and knowledge.

In the northwest, between Fall and Winter, is a solemn feast honoring the family's dead ancestors. Carved turnips, candles, and food are left outside for any wandering spirits. Everyone huddles next to

*the hearth, wondering, fearing, and dreading the long cold Winter to
come.*

*The wheel slowly rotates so that each scene passes by you. And
in the distance, at the central hub of the wheel, you notice two figures. Because of the light and their distance, you cannot tell anything about them. But you know that they are there. And that is
enough.*

The most common Wiccan calendar is loosely based on a
nineteenth-century reconstruction of the ancient Irish Coligny
calendar. In its current form, it is divided into quarter and cross-
quarter days. Quarter days mark the solstices and equinoxes of
the solar year, thus dividing it into four equal quarters. Cross-
quarter days are based on the pastoral calendar of planting and
animal husbandry as practiced in the British Isles. They are called
"cross-quarter" days because they fall midway between each of the
quarter days, so that there is a sabbat every six weeks. Because
the cross-quarter days were the ones originally recognized on the
ancient calendar, we'll start with them.

The Cross Quarters

The earliest known Irish calendar divided the year into two
halves: Summer and Winter, light and dark. The light of Summer
began on May 1 and ended October 31. The dark of Winter began
on November 1 and ended April 30. Because it was believed that
life begins in darkness, either in the womb, or in the cool dark
soil, each day began at sunset rather than at midnight. Thus,
Beltane or May Day actually began at sunset on April 30, and
Samhain or Halloween actually began at sunset on October 31.

The name "Beltane" comes from the words *Bel Tinne*, meaning
"fire of the God Bel." Samhain comes from the word *Samanos*,
and means "end of Summer." Both were considered in-between or
liminal times, falling into neither Summer nor Winter, and thus

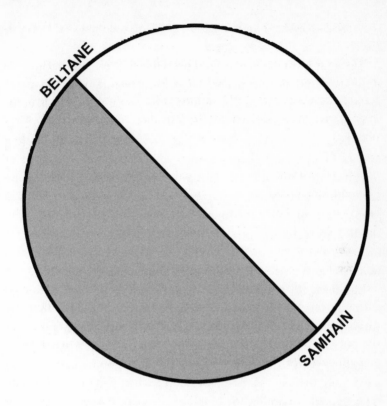

were magical times when the veil between the world of the living and the world of the spirits was thin and able to be crossed. It was a time to commune with the dead, seek cooperation with the spirits of nature, and see into the future. Many Irish tales of Otherworldly encounters, including Cuchulainn's encounter with the green giant and Oisin's journey to the land of youth, occur on these two dates. Also, since both days were between the worlds, normal social conventions no longer applied and people were free to experiment with other lifestyles. Peasants could be king for a day and rulers could escape the bonds of social propriety and act undignified. Excessive eating and drinking, extramarital sex, cross-dressing, and a wide range of indulgences were allowed.

The year is divided again to represent the cycles of the agricultural year. Imbolg (February 2) marks the beginning of the planting and growing season. Six months later, on Lughnasadh (August 2) the harvesting and dying season begins.

Imbolg, which means "in the bag" and refers to the expanding udders of pregnant sheep, is also sometimes called Oimelc or "ewe's milk." One of the early signs of approaching Spring in an agricultural society is the "bagging up" of the ewes with milk in preparation of lamb birthing. To honor the growing daylight, candles were lit to spread the illumination, rituals were performed to ease the birthing, and prayers were offered up for a bountiful and productive Spring and Summer.

Lughnasadh, which means "Lugh's assembly," corresponded with the largest "oenach" or country fair in Ireland. In early August, the first crops of the harvest are ready to be gathered, but the harvest isn't in full swing yet. This makes it a perfect time to gather with other farmers to exchange goods, catch up on news, and do business. Also, for people who lived in the hills with their extended families for much of the year, it was a chance for the teenagers to meet someone outside of the bloodline for a possible mate. Cooking contests, animal judging, and feats of strength were all ways to assess the householding and farming skills of a prospective mate. Thus, Lughnasadh was also a traditional time of marriages. Even today, if you go to a modern-day country fair, you will see how little things have changed. There are still the blue-ribbon contests, the animal judging competitions, vendors selling equipment and goods, and swarms of teenagers all checking each other out. Old habits die hard.

The overlaying of these two sets of cycles—Summer/Winter, planting/harvesting—divides the year into quarters, each with varying degrees of light and darkness. The period from Samhain to Imbolg is the darkest period, where the darkness of Winter

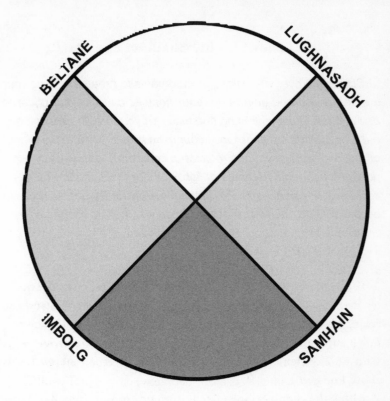

meets the harvesting and dying season. Everything in this period is about contraction, sleep, and death. The period between Beltane and Lughnasadh is just the opposite. The light of summer meets the planting and growing season, making everything in this period about expansion, activity, and life. The periods of Imbolg to Beltane and from Lughnasadh to Samhain are shadow times, each marking the twilight time between the depths of darkness and the heights of light. As we saw in the previous chapter, liminal times and spaces such as these are especially useful for divination and other magickal workings.

Meditation: Light, Shadow, and Dark

Close your eyes and take a few moments to breathe, feeling your breath coming and going from your nostrils, causing your chest to rise and fall. Quiet your mind and focus on your breath, relaxing any parts of you that are tight. Once your mind is quiet, picture the Wheel of the Year with its various regions of light, dark, and shadow. How do you feel during the times of light? Of dark? Of shadow? Reflect on where in the year you are right now. Are your life and activities in accord with the season? If not, how can you make it such?

Quarter Days

While the cross-quarter days mark the pastoral year, the quarter days mark the progression of the sun across the sky and the relative amounts of daylight it brings. Because the sun is the primary source of all active, vitiating energy, its cycle provides us with an excellent gauge of how our own internal energy levels should be going.

Litha, the Summer Solstice, falls on or around June 21. Being the longest day of the year, our energy levels are high and moving outward. We become extra busy and stay up later because the sun is still up. We focus more outwardly at this time of year by attending more social activities such as barbeques, ball games, and family reunions. Even when we stay home, we focus on the outward side of our homes and lives, painting the house, mowing the lawn, and planting gardens. Except for occasional sunbathing and reading, more of our energy is directed toward reflecting outward and "doing," rather than reflecting inward and just "being."

Yule, the Winter Solstice, occurs around December 21. Being the shortest day of the year, our energies are just the opposite from Litha. We feel the need to sit quietly and focus inward in reflection. Even when we gather socially, it is more of a cocooning in intimate gatherings around the hearth with close friends than huge blowouts.

This is one reason why our culture experiences so much stress and depression around the holidays. Our culture's perpetual obsession with a youthful, summery attitude insists that we keep up the summer pace all year long. For Yuletide, we're expected to rush around buying gifts, throwing and attending parties, and attending concerts. This tension between our natural instinct (and nostalgia) for a quieter, more intimate Yuletide and cultural expectations is what contributes to the holiday blues.

At the equinoxes (March 21, Ostara, and September 21, Mabon), the energies of Summer's outward, vital expansion and Winter's inward, nurturing contraction are in balance. These are the times to finish up and put away the work of the previous phase and begin the next. Traditionally, this is reflected in "Spring Cleaning," where we clean out the dust and accumulations from Winter and get ready for Summer. Likewise, in the Fall we tidy up our yards and gardens and button up our houses in preparation for Winter. Psychologically and psychically, we need to do the same at these times of year.

By placing the quarters and cross-quarters on a diagram together, several things become apparent. First, even though mainstream culture calls the Summer Solstice the first day of Summer, and the Winter Solstice the first day of Winter, the solstices and equinoxes actually mark the midpoints of the seasons of light, dark, and shadow. That is why some Wiccans refer to the Summer Solstice as Midsummer, and the Winter Solstice as Midwinter.

Second, these midpoints are turning points in each season. Ostara marks the height of the Shadow time, the mixing of light and darkness. But it isn't simply a switch that turns the Wheel to the next season. Each season is a spectrum of growing or declining light and darkness/planting and harvesting. Therefore, although Imbolg marks the beginning of Shadow time, it is mostly

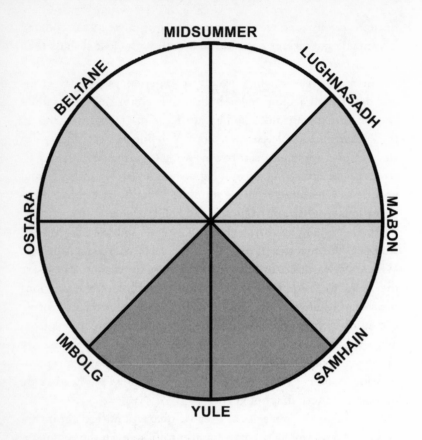

dark with just a hint of light in contrast to Beltane, which is mostly light with just a hint of darkness. Similarly, Beltane is the beginning of the fully Light time, but these energies do not peak until Midsummer, when they again start to wane until Lughnasadh. Lastly, the pairs of Beltane and Lughnasadh, and Samhain and Imbolg have much in common with each other. Beltane and Lughnasadh are both at the borders of Light and Shadow times. Similarly, Imbolg and Samhain border the Dark and Shadow times. The significance of this is best illustrated by looking at them in the light of life cycles.

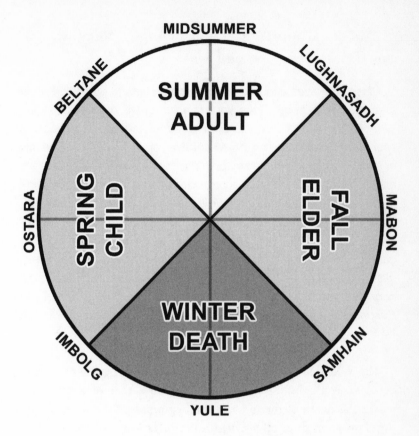

If we see Spring as the time of childhood, Summer as corresponding with adulthood, Fall as old age, and Winter as death, then we see that Imbolg and Samhain mark the gates of life. Birth is at Imbolg and death is at Samhain. Similarly, Beltane and Lughnasadh mark the change in and out of adulthood. At Beltane we stop being children and become adults. At Lughnasadh we stop being adults and move into elderhood. These have strong implications for possible rituals for these holidays and will have further significance as we add in some of the other mythic cycles.

Meditation: Life Stages of Light, Shadow, and Dark

Close your eyes and take a few deep breaths to quiet your mind and relax your body. Once your mind is quiet, picture again the Wheel of the Year divided into Light, Shadow, and Dark times. Locate your current light stage on the Wheel. Are you in the Light or Shadow of life? Given what you know about the quarters and cross-quarters, are your current life activities appropriate for your place on the Wheel? If you are in the Summer of your life, are your activities mostly out-wardly focused on career and social obligations or are you out of synch in some way, perhaps still focusing on Springtime fun and games? Now, starting from where you currently are on the Wheel, picture how your life should change to be in accord with each sea-son. See yourself growing older and your life moving from Light Summer, to early harvest, to Shadow Fall, to eventually Darkness. How does it feel to go through these stages?

The Wheel symbolically represents the entire cycle of human experience. Beginning on the Wiccan New Year of Samhain, it marks the death of the old and the beginning of the darkest sea-son. However, since all life begins in the darkness of the womb, it is a time of hope and new starts. Thus, one of the traditional ac-tivities at Samhain was to divine the prospects of the coming cycle.

Yule is the longest and darkest night of the year. However, it also marks the turning of the tide toward darkness and the slow increase of light again. Thus, it truly is the birth of the sun. The lighting of a candle or Yule log symbolizes that return of light.

Imbolg marks the very first signs that Spring will come. Al-though the grass is still buried under the snow, the days are no-ticeably longer and the ewes are beginning to show signs of giving birth soon. Hope is in the air.

Ostara is the equinox. The number of minutes of light each day has now caught up with night. All is in balance for now, but because of the increase in light, the energy will become more active and outward from this point on. This is a good time to refocus one's balance, clean out the old—Spring cleaning for the house and fasting and cleansing for the body—and prepare for the next stage.

Beltane marks Spring in full swing. The grass is green, the lambs are born, the new seeds are being planted, and the whole world seems young and full of promise. In keeping with an agricultural theme, this is a good time to plant the seeds of growth for the rest of the year, sow some wild oats, and celebrate the fertility of the earth.

Litha is the Summer Solstice and the longest day of the year. Human activity is at its peak. We are most active and outgoing during this time. It is a celebration of being alive and interacting with the world at large.

Lughnasadh marks the first harvest of our labors of the Spring and Summer. We celebrate and share our bounty, make the most of the last days of Summer, and prepare for the coming Fall.

Mabon is the Fall Equinox. Again, the amount of daylight and darkness are equal, but now the darkness is on the rise. This is again a time to focus on balance like at Ostara, cleaning out the old from Summer, and preparing for the next stage.

Samhain marks the end of the cycle. In the British Isles, this was traditionally the time when the men who had been in the fields all Summer brought the flocks home for the Winter. It was a time for reunion and celebration. It was also the time of the animal slaughter and the last preparations before the long, dark, and sometimes dangerous Winter. Because it was a liminal time, when the spirits could pass from their world to ours, it was also a time to honor the dead.

The Goddess and the Green Man

Close your eyes. Picture in your mind a young couple, children really. They are walking the boundaries of a giant circle, the Wheel of the Year. It is early Spring with the green grass just peaking up through patches in the snow. Melting snow runs in rivulets into small, babbling streams. The very earliest flowers, the crocus, add yellow and purple clusters against the white backdrop of snow. The girl is dressed in a simple white dress with green trim. The boy is dressed in pants and shirt, all of green.

As they walk the Wheel, early Spring turns to the bright green and plethora of flowers, birds, and bees of full Spring. The girl has become a beautiful young woman, fully developed. The boy has become a young man, still all clad in green, with the beginnings of a beard on his face.

Spring yields to Summer and the young woman has blossomed into motherhood, first with full belly and breasts, and later with babe in arms. The young man in green has now matured and holds in his calloused hands the tools of his trade.

As Summer yields to Fall, the babe grows and leaves. The mother, strong from her years carrying and caring for her children, now begins to stoop. Her hair becomes gray, and wrinkles appear on her once smooth face. She is still beautiful, but now it is the beauty of wisdom, experience, and caring. The man has aged as well. He has now changed his clothes from the green of Summer to the bright red of Fall and the harvest. He, too, has become strong from his years of work. His sun-weathered face now has deep crevasses and his hair is streaked with gray. He is still handsome, but his attractiveness, too, is due to his wisdom, experience, and caring.

With the first snows of Winter, the Lady, her hair now the brilliant white of snow, dresses in her white night gown. She lies on the earth and quietly falls asleep as the snow covers her like a blanket. The old man has donned robes of red and green. In his white beard and hair he has hung ivy, holly, and mistletoe. Around his waist he has a belt strewn with various herbs and plants. In a bag that he carries over his shoulder, he carries treasures unseen. He spends the winter walking the forests, checking on the plants, the animals, and the Lady during their long winter sleep. He is the Old Man of the Woods.

As the snow begins to melt again, the Lady arises from her slumber. She is again a young girl, a child in white robes. And she is joined once again by the young boy. They take each other's hands and begin the journey anew.

Drawn from an obscure family tradition of Wicca, this mythic calendar is one of my favorites. The Goddess rules the nine months from Imbolg to Samhain, symbolic of the human gestational period. The God rules the three months from Samhain to Imbolg. That is not to say that the Goddess is not present in one of her forms during the God's term, nor he during her reign, just that their influence is less.

The Goddess's nine-month reign, corresponding to the Shadow and Light times of the year, is divided into three smaller divisions of three months each. Each division, symbolic of the early, middle, and end trimesters of a pregnancy, is associated with the stages of the Goddess: Maiden, Mother, and Crone. Thus, from Imbolg to Beltane is Maiden time, corresponding with the Shadow time of Spring and childhood, from Beltane to Lughnasadh is Mother time, corresponding with the peak of Light time and the height of Summer, and from Lughnasadh to Samhain is Crone time, corresponding to the Shadow time of Fall and elderhood. During the God's reign, she is the Sleeping Winter Queen. Notice how these correspond perfectly with the four seasons and human life stages.

In turn, each three-month-long division of the Goddess time is again split into three one-month-long divisions, again associated with the three stages of Maiden, Mother, and Crone. Thus, each month of the Goddess's nine-month reign has a dual designation. From February 1 to March 1 would be the beginning or Maiden

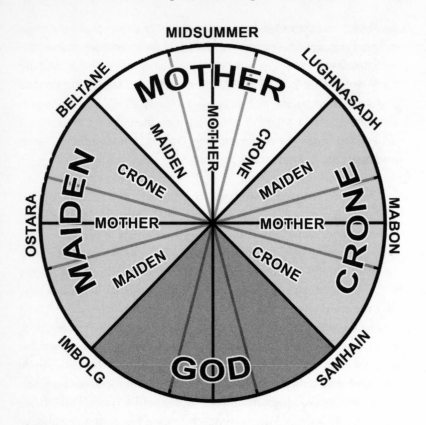

month of the Maiden time. July 1 to August 1 would be the ending or Crone month of the Mother time. The monthly subdivisions show how everything, from the cycles of nature to the lifespan of humans, can be broken into successive stages of beginning, middle, and end.

Meditation: Maidens, Mothers, and Crones

Spend some time meditating on what it means to be a maiden, a mother, and a crone. Then meditate on what it means to be a maid-

enly, beginning crone versus a motherly, mature crone, or the elder crone. What about an elderly mother? How do each of these nine distinctions vary and how do they reflect differently in the calendar and the stages of our lives? Why doesn't the God have a similar nine phases?

The God's reign, corresponding with the Dark time of Winter and death from Samhain to Imbolg, is not divided into smaller divisions. He does not go through the same cycles as the Goddess. Instead, he has his own roles in relationship to each of her phases. Being the God of vegetation, from Imbolg to Beltane (the Goddess's Maiden time), he is the Young Green Man. It is the Young Green Man who matures from child to young adult and at Beltane mates with the Maiden, beginning her phase of the Mother. From Beltane to Lughnasadh, he is the Mature Green Man serving as companion and consort to the Mother. He is the lushness of Summertime in preparation for the harvest. From Lughnasadh to Samhain he is the Red Man, God of the harvest. His red color is symbolic of the changing leaves and the red blood of animals slaughtered for food. From Samhain to Imbolg, while the Goddess is asleep, he rules alone as the Old Man of the Woods. He is the wild, solitary wise man dispensing the gifts of herbs, potions, and wisdom to all he meets.

Notice how the solstices and equinoxes always fall into the Mother subdivisions. Ostara is during the Mother month of the Maiden time. Midsummer is during the Mother month of the Mother time, and Mabon is during the Mother month of the Crone time. Yule falls in the middle month of the God time, which technically is not a Mother time, but it still shows its place in the middle of the cycle. This reinforces what we already know about the quarters, namely, that they represent the midpoints of the seasons rather than the beginnings. But more important, they mark the peak times when a seasonal energy is at its strongest and most mature. This is ritually important because if you are going to do a

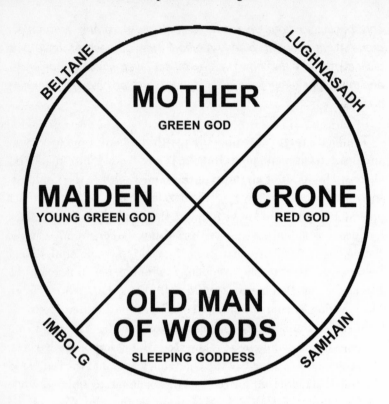

ritual working with a particular seasonal energy, for example, the vigorous growth of Spring, you need to do your ritual on or just before Ostara to catch the Spring energy at its peak. If you wait until after April 1, the Spring energy will have moved into its crone phase, waning and starting to transform into the next stage.

Cross-quarter days (Imbolg, Beltane, Lughnasadh, and Samhain) mark the Crone or end of one cycle and the beginning or Maiden phase of another. At the same time, the God is also changing his aspect. Imbolg marks the beginning of the Young Maiden and Young Green Man's reign. At Beltane the Young Mother and Mature Green Man come to power, passing it on to the Young Crone and the Red God at Lughnasadh, and eventually abdicating to the Sleeping White Goddess and the Old Man at Samhain. Again, these images have uses in ritual and spellwork. Traditionally, the cross-quarter days have been considered the best times to do magick. We can now see that it is because they mark that time when one age is passing away and the next is beginning—the perfect time to plant seeds of change. Thus, quarter days are ritually useful for tapping into an existing seasonal energy while cross-quarters are specifically about new directions and new beginnings.

Similarly, by being aware of how each month reflects the powers of nature as symbolized by the Goddess and the Green Man, we can attune ourselves to those energies and harmonize ourselves with the Divine Will. The monthly God and Goddess phases are:

January	Winter God/Sleeping Goddess
February	Young Maiden/Young Green God
March	Mature Maiden/Young Green God
April	Elder Maiden/Young Green God
May	Young Mother/Mature Green God
June	Mature Mother/Mature Green God
July	Elder Mother/Mature Green God
August	Young Crone/Red God
September	Mature Crone/Red God
October	Elder Crone/Red God
November	Winter God/Sleeping Goddess
December	Winter God/Sleeping Goddess

Meditation: Monthly Energies

On the first day of each month, spend several minutes meditating on the phase of the Goddess and God for the coming month. For ex-

ample, in August you would meditate on the images of the Young Crone and the Red God. Think about ways in which you can align your life with and use their natural energies?

The Kings of Darkness and Light

Close your eyes and picture a giant circle. This time there are two different figures standing opposite each other. On the northern side is the King of Darkness. He is dressed all in black armor, a dark helmet covering his face entirely. His eyes, burning like small fires, shine out through the eye slits in his helmet. In his left hand he holds a great black sword. On his right arm is a shield so dark that it seems to suck the light out of the very air.

On the southern side stands the King of Light. The light shining from his armor makes it hard to even look at him, however, it appears that he is dressed all in golden armor. A brilliant helmet covers his entire face save for eye slits that reveal dark orbs somehow not illuminated by his light. In his right hand he holds a great golden sword. On his left arm is a brilliant shield seemingly made of light itself.

The Kings of Light and Darkness is one of two mythic calendars drawn from British Traditional Witchcraft. This calendar is based on the ebb and flow of relative daylight and darkness during the year. In this regard, the myth focuses primarily on the stages of development of the kings. The Goddess is the never-changing earth from which all things are born. She is the mother of us all.

The Kings of Light and Darkness are in a never-ending battle over rule of the year. During the course of the year, each king is conceived from the union of the Earth Goddess and the other king. Each king is born, grows, takes rule over six months of the year from equinox to equinox, dies, and is conceived and reborn again. How this plays out during the Wheel of the Year is as follows:

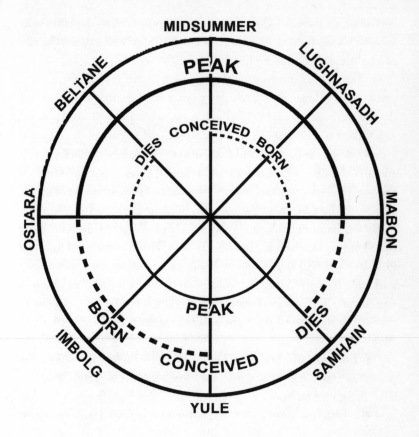

The King of Light is conceived on Yule (December 21), the middle of the Dark time and under the rule of the Old Man. This being the Winter Solstice, it is the longest night of the year, but it also marks the beginning of the return of the light. This holiday is usually a celebration of the darkness, but it includes the lighting of a single candle to symbolize the spark of life that will give birth to the light once again.

On Imbolg (February 2), the King of Light is born along with the Young Maiden and the beginning of Shadow time. He is one and the same as the Young Green Man. This day, also known by its Christian name of Candlemas, is a celebration of the birth and growth of the light. From the one candle lit at Yule comes the ritual lighting of many candles.

By the Spring Equinox (March 21), the King of Light is fully grown and takes reign. This day marks the fact that the hours of daylight are now equal to, and will soon exceed, the hours of night.

On Beltane (April 30), the King of Light becomes the Mature Green Man and the Goddess moves into her phase as the Mature Mother. The King of Darkness, who has continued to diminish in power as the daylight grows and the nighttime shrinks, dies just when the last shadows are banished by the Light time.

By Midsummer (June 21), the middle of Light time, the King of Light has reached his peak of power. The days are hot and the longest they will be. While at his peak, the King of Light mates with the Mature Mother Goddess and the King of Darkness is conceived. For just in reverse of Yule, the longest day of the year marks the decline of the light and the coming of the dark half of the year.

On Lughnasadh (August 2), the King of Light moves into his phase as Red God of the harvest alongside the Crone Goddess. The King of Darkness is reborn just as the light begins to fade into the Shadow time and the decline of the year becomes more evident.

On the Fall Equinox (Sept. 21), the King of Darkness is fully grown and takes his reign back from the King of Light. The hours of day and night are equal again but from this point onward, darkness will exceed the light.

On Samhain (October 31), the beginning of the Dark time, the King of Light, who has continued to diminish in power as the nighttime grows and the daylight dwindles, dies. He enters the Underworld, ruled by the Old Man, and awaits rebirth in Spring.

On Yule, the King of Darkness reaches the peak of his power. The nights are the longest of the year. While at his peak, the King of Darkness unites with the Goddess while she sleeps and the King of Light is conceived again. The cycle begins again.

From this then, we can see that the King of Light is really the king of the Overworld, the world of light and living things. He is the Green and Red God. Conversely, the King of Darkness is king of the Underworld, when the world is dark, sleeping, or dead. It is the King of Darkness who is the Old Man. It is for this reason that when the King of Light dies and travels to the Underworld, the year is under the sway of the Old Man. Similarly, when the King of Darkness is dead, the Green God is at his peak. Thus, they represent the two complimentary, opposing forces of nature—light and life versus darkness and death. By reflecting on this imagery, you should be able to create a number of powerful meditations and seasonal rituals reflecting the epic forces of birth, life, and rebirth.

Meditation: Kings

Close your eyes and take a few moments to breathe, feeling your breath coming and going from your nostrils, causing your chest to rise and fall. Quiet your mind and focus on your breath, relaxing any parts of you that are tight. Once your mind is quiet, picture yourself floating in the void, an endless darkness. You see a spark of light in the distance. The light grows larger and larger. Suddenly, you burst into a world of bright light and large fuzzy shapes. You are born. As you grow, you notice a dark man around you. As you grow into a child, the man seems to grow into an old man. On Beltane, the day that you become a man, he dies. You continue to grow stronger. On the longest day of the year, you make love to a beautiful woman and she conceives a baby. The baby, a dark haired and dark skinned child, is born on the first day of harvest tide. As you slip slowly into elderhood, the baby grows into a child and eventually a dark young man. On Samhain, you say good-bye to your fully grown son and pass back into the void. What lessons have you learned about life, death, and the cycles of nature?

The Oak King and the Holly King

Close your eyes. Picture in your mind a great circle spreading out horizontally to the corners of the universe. Standing at one end of the circle is a figure. He is dressed in flowing green robes, the color of leaves and grass. His beard and hair are golden, like spun sunshine. His bright, lively eyes are the color of the sky on a clear Spring day. In his hand he carries a staff of oak, the top of which is still sprouting leaves. Woven into his hair is a crown of green oak leaves. He is the Oak King.

Standing at the opposite end of the circle is another figure. This man is dressed in brown robes, the color of the trees once the leaves have all fallen. His beard and hair are jet black like the sky on a cold Winter night. His gray piercing eyes remind you of the steely gray clouds on a late November day. In his hand he carries a silver sickle as if fresh from the harvest. Woven into his hair he wears a crown of sharp, waxy leaves and red berries. He is the Holly King.

The story of the Oak King and the Holly King is also drawn from British Traditional Witchcraft. It is a solar-based myth representing the waxing and waning of the sun and its effects and interactions with the Goddess and the natural world. It describes the eternal competition between these two Gods for the favor of the Earth Goddess.

Unlike the Kings of Light and Dark, the Holly King and the Oak King each grows and controls only half of the year. The Oak King reigns over the waxing or growing part of the year. Thus, his term is Yule until Midsummer. The Oak King is born at Yule, the peak of the Old Man of the Wood's reign. As the Young Green God, he slowly grows in strength, while in the natural world the light grows and Dark time and Shadow time fades.

Reaching his peak at Beltane, the beginning of the Light time, he mates with the Young Mother, giving her his entire life force so that he dies in her embrace. She in turn resurrects him as the Mature Green God. His power fades quickly thereafter until he dies at Midsummer.

The Holly King reigns over the waning or declining part of the year. His term begins with being born at Midsummer, the peak of the Mature Green Man's reign. The Holly King quickly grows in strength during the fading of the Light time. Where the Oak King reached his peak near the end of his term, the Holly King reaches his at Lughnasadh, near the beginning of his reign. On this date, with Shadow time just beginning, he mates with the Young Crone, giving her his entire life force so that he dies in her embrace. She in turn resurrects him as the Red God. His power slowly fades through the rest of the year, from Shadow time and into Dark time, until he dies at Yule.

As shown by their frequent use in Alexandrian circles, the Oak and Holly Kings' cycle provides multiple opportunities to meditate on the themes of life and death and how they are reflected in the relationship between the movements of the sun and the natural world.

Meditation: Holly and Oak

Quiet your mind and focus on your breath, relaxing any parts of you that are tight. When you are ready, bring into your mind everything you remember about the Oak King and Beltane. Reflect on why he matures slowly from Yule to Beltane and then dies quickly. What insights do you gain about the cycles of life and death by meditating on his ritual death mating at Beltane? Similarly, why does the Holly King mature quickly and die slowly? Why does he mate with the Goddess on Lughnasadh? If necessary, bring the images of these kings into your mind and ask them these questions. What do they tell you?

The Zodiac

Close your eyes. Picture yourself inside of a giant globe. You sit in the center while the images on the surface of it whirl about you. You see many symbols: a fiery Ram, a Crab seemingly made of water, and a Bull made out of rock. Some of the images, like the Twins, seem to be ever shifting. Others, like the Scorpio, seem stable and solid. Still others, like the Fish-tailed Seagoat of Capricorn, seem to move in jumps and starts. All of them whirl and dance in front of you. Notice how each of them makes you feel. If you know your own sign, take a moment to see it, talk to it, and learn from it. If you also know which sign the sun is in right now, focus on that sign as well.

There are twelve signs of the Zodiac. Each sign begins approximately on the twenty-first of each month, beginning with Aries at the Spring Equinox (March 21). Each sign is associated with an element and a quality. The elements are: Fire, Earth, Air, and Water. Fire signs tend to be active, energetic, spontaneous, quick, and initiating. Earth signs tend to be passive, stable, solid, and grounded. Air signs tend to be active, communicative, intellectual, and abstract. Water signs tend to be passive, creative, fluidic, receptive, and sustaining.

The qualities are: cardinal, fixed, and mutable. Cardinal signs can be active, independent, ambitious, mentally quick, impetuous, and domineering. Fixed signs can be stable, accumulative, persevering, obstinate, and stuck in their ways. Mutable signs can be adaptable, subtle, intuitive, versatile, mentally quick and clever, unreliable, and deceptive.

Aries (March 21–April 19) Cardinal Fire
Taurus (April 20–May 20) Fixed Earth
Gemini (May 21–June 20) Mutable Air
Cancer (June 21–July 22) Cardinal Water

Leo (July 23–August 22) Fixed Fire
Virgo (August 23–September 22) Mutable Earth
Libra (September 23–October 22) Cardinal Air
Scorpio (October 23–November 21) Fixed Water
Sagittarius (November 22–December 21) Mutable Fire
Capricorn (December 22–January 19) Cardinal Earth
Aquarius (January 20–February 18) Fixed Air
Pisces (February 19–March 20) Mutable Water

Notice how each quarter day corresponds with a cardinal sign, marking a new astrological beginning. Yule, which corresponds

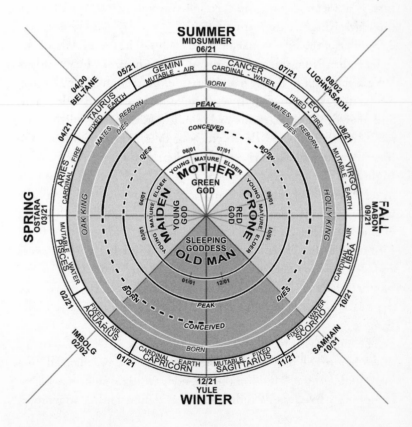

with the beginning of the cardinal earth sign of Capricorn, is the day on which the Oak King is born and the King of Light is conceived. While Yule is the middle of Dark time, it marks the pivotal point where the darkness begins to wane and light begins to grow. The Old Man of the Woods' reign and the sleep of the White Queen are halfway over. It is the beginning of the end.

Conversely, Midsummer, which corresponds with the beginning of the cardinal Water sign of Cancer, is the day on which the Holly King is born and the King of Darkness is conceived. It marks the peak of light and the beginning of the growth of the darkness. Ostara, marked by the cardinal Fire sign of Aries, begins the Light King's reign, which lasts until Mabon, which in turn is associated with the cardinal Air sign of Libra and when the Dark King's reign begins.

Similarly, the cross-quarter days each fall in the middle of the fixed signs. From this we can surmise that the cross-quarter days have something to do with stability and/or accumulation. In particular, they have to do with accumulation of steady development and growth. They mark major life milestones such as birth, marriage, retirement, and death. Imbolg falls in the middle of the fixed Air sign of Aquarius and marks the birth of the King of Light and the growing strength of the Oak King. Beltane falls into the middle of the fixed Earth sign of Taurus. On this day the Oak King mates, dies, and is reborn. At the same time, the King of Darkness dies. Lughnasadh falls into the middle of the fixed Fire sign of Leo. This date marks the birth of the King of Darkness and also the marriage, death, and rebirth of the Holly King. Lastly, Samhain falls in the fixed Water sign of Scorpio. This day marks the death of the King of Light and the final decline of the Holly King.

The mutable signs mark that time where the old starts to break down before the new begins. There are no holidays that fall during mutable signs. Thus, on the calendar cardinal signs mark new beginnings, fixed signs indicate consolidation and commemoration of those new accomplishments, and the mutable signs show the period of chaotic of adaptation and experimentation that takes place before a new beginning. They represent the transition period between when a developmental stage is attained and the beginning of the new stage. The mutable Water sign of Pisces corresponds with the last month of the King of Darkness's reign and the Light King's growth into rulership. The mutable air sign of Gemini marks the last month of the Oak King's life and the period between when the Dark King has died and when he is conceived again. The mutable Earth sign of Virgo is the converse of Pisces in that now the Light King's reign is ending and the Dark King is waxing in strength. And the mutable Fire sign of Sagittarius, like Beltane, marks the last month of the Holly King's life and the period between when the Light King has died and when he is again conceived.

However, we have to be careful not to take these beginnings, milestones, and endings too rigidly. Note that the cross-quarter holidays, which fall in the middle of the fixed signs, mark the beginnings of the Light, Shadow, and Dark times and the corresponding Maiden, Mother, Crone, and Old Man phases. The cardinal signs and their corresponding quarter holidays fall into the middle of the Mother phases. This is because the cycles of the Kings of Darkness and Light and the myth of the Holly and Oak Kings are all solar-based mythic cycles. That is, they correspond with what the sun is doing. That is why they all begin their various phases according to the solstices and equinoxes. However, the Goddess phase cycle is based on the pastoral calendar just as are the cross-quarter holidays. This should be taken into consideration when creating rituals and spells that mix mythic themes.

The Wheel Comes 'Round

By meditating and thinking about these various mythic themes, it is possible to get some deep insights into the calendar and how it reflects our various life stages. In turn, we can use these insights to create rituals and spells to harmonize our lives with these cycles. For example, a meditation could be written exploring why Beltane, while often thought of as a day of life and vitality, is the date for the deaths of both the King of Darkness and the Oak King. Or a ritual exploring why Lughnasadh marks both the birth of the King of Darkness and the death of the Holly King. Perhaps a meditation on the significance of the Oak King mating with the Mother while the Holly King mates with the Crone? When combined with one another, the complex myths and symbols of these various cycles can provide an endless supply of opportunities for insight.

An adept is attuned to the cycles of nature in all the places that they express themselves, including our bodies, relationships, and lives. By attuning yourself to the major seasonal forces surrounding you, you are ready to move on to the next step in the circle of knowledge. You are ready to begin harnessing the energies around you, adjust them into harmony with the natural cycles, and use them for healing yourself and others.

CHAPTER 5

Heal, Hale, Holy:
Healing and Spellworking

A n adept is healthy and can create health in others. The previous chapter was about observing the forces of nature
around you and by attuning to them, moving toward harmonizing your life with them. Now we will study how the forces of nature move within your body and how, by harmonizing them, to
create holistic health. This is one more step in bringing yourself
into alignment with the Divine will.

A popular bumper sticker proclaims "Witches Heal" and indeed, most Wiccans do some kind of healing work as part of their
spiritual practice. However, to move beyond the basic level of
raising a little generalized energy and giving to the afflicted person in need, an adept needs to have a deeper knowledge of how
energy moves in the body, how to recognize imbalances, and
based on those findings, what strategies can be employed to rem-
edy them. Essentially, an adept needs to know how to become a
holistic healer. This chapter is divided into three sections. The first
section covers the basic definitions and concepts around healing,
energy, and pathology. The second section goes deeply into various diagnostic techniques; how they are performed, and how their
findings are interpreted. Lastly, section three explores how treatment strategies can be matched to the diagnostic findings.

Definitions and Concepts

Before we proceed too far, it is important that we define some general and specific terms and concepts of healing. We will explore the concepts of:

1. Health and illness
2. Symptomatic versus holistic healing
3. How whole is holistic healing
4. Energy and energy work

Health and Illness

At all times there exists a spectrum of levels of health. It runs from being truly "healthy" on one end to being "ill with symptoms" on the other. In between, these two extremes are varying levels of "ill without symptoms."

Healthy ⟷ Ill Without Symptoms ⟷ Ill with Symptoms

Healthy means just what it says. It is optimal wellness where all the body's functions and organs are working efficiently, effectively, and harmoniously. There is no dysfunction or illness of any kind. Very few adults in Western society qualify as truly healthy.

Ill without symptoms is the state where there is a dysfunction in one or more systems of the body but no major symptoms have manifested yet. We are sliding toward being "sick" but aren't showing symptoms or at least aren't showing symptoms severe enough to notice or address. Ill without symptoms applies to times when our immune system is down but we haven't caught anything—yet. Or it might be when our gallbladder is filling with small stones that aren't big or numerous enough to cause pain. The most extreme case, of course, is when the body is generating precancerous cells. From a holistic perspective, the growth of such cells is due to an imbalance in the body that has existed for some time. Over weeks, months, or years, this imbalance gradually leads to growth of these mutant cells until one day, there are enough to tip the scales dramatically and suddenly it looks as if cancer has sprung up overnight. Really, however, the problem has been building for a long time and, if it had been corrected early enough, could have been prevented. Almost the entire population of Western adults falls into this category. And more commonly, many of these people *do* have symptoms; they just are ignoring them or attributing them to something else.

Ill with symptoms is exactly as it sounds. Once a person is "sick," he or she goes to get medication, surgery, or some other care to make the symptoms go away. But this is precisely the problem. The typical approach is to go and get something that simply makes the symptoms go away, but never addresses the real underlying problem. We just take something to push us back into ill without symptoms and await the next flare-up or variation on the problem. No one with a chronic migraine has a deficiency of migraine medications. No one with allergies has too little Allegra in their diet. These medicines just mask the underlying imbalance. A true healer is always seeking to find the underlying problem, hopefully before symptoms occur, and to return the person to health and not just hide the symptoms.

Symptomatic Healing vs. Holistic

When it comes to healing, there are two general approaches: symptomatic and holistic. The symptomatic approach focuses on the specific, localized problem and tries to address it directly. If you have a pain in your gallbladder, the symptomatic approach would be to take scans and x-rays of the organ and look for stones or other dysfunctions. If a physical problem is found, we'll continue to use gallstones as an example, then surgery would be performed to remove the gallbladder. If no obvious answer is found, medications and diet might be prescribed to address the symptomatic pain, and the offending organ might still be removed just for good measure. In more generalized conditions such as fibromyalgia, rheumatoid arthritis, and Lyme disease, pain management medications might be prescribed. Each of these strategies focuses solely on the symptom and attempts treatment strategies that specifically address that symptom to make it go away. The goal is to be "without symptoms," not necessarily to be healthy as we defined it.

The holistic approach sees each person as a whole unit. You are not just your gallbladder, or your lungs, or your heart, and they do not operate independently from one another. You are a connected whole. So when one part of you starts to become out of balance, the rest of your body adjusts to compensate for it. A problem anywhere in your body will affect the entire functioning of the rest of your body. Thus, a holistic practitioner will look at the whole person to get a full picture of what is compensating where, and ultimately, what underlying imbalance is causing the problem. So, if someone presents with a chronic tennis elbow but also tends to be constipated, has occasional allergies, and has athlete's foot, a holistic healer will look at this pattern of symptoms and try to find the underlying common cause for all of them. In this case, the common cause could be a problem with water metabolism and distribution. When it comes to treatment, it is this underlying cause that will be the primary focus with only a little bit of attention given to the specific symptoms to make them tolerable until the underlying problem is cleared. When people visit a holistic healer for a specific problem, they often find that all their other symptoms also disappear.

How Whole Is Holistic Healing

Holistic healing is more than just physical symptoms. Holistic healing sees each person as a whole, unique individual formed and continually influenced by every aspect of his or her life—past, present, and future.

Each of us was born with particular genetic predispositions. We are stronger in some areas and weaker in others based on the genes and energetic qualities passed on to us from our ancestors. On top of that, we have a full life until the present moment of experiences, influences, and events. What we ate, what we were taught, how we felt, events and experiences that influenced us, how we think about those events, things that have been done to us and things we have done to ourselves—everything that has happened to us in our past has shaped us into the person we are at this exact moment. This is our current underlying condition.

Based on those past influences, we have created our current state. This includes not only our physical state but also our mental state, our environment of relationships with friends, family, and lovers, our jobs, possessions, and patterns and choices in how we eat and live in our world. And these choices will either ameliorate or aggravate our current underlying condition. For example, I might have an underlying tendency to getting internally overheated, manifesting externally as migraines and acne. This may be the result of genetic weakness but also a past poor diet and certain life traumas. I have created a busy life for myself, surrounded by the hum of a highly stimulating urban environment, and an active work and social life that leaves too little time for quiet or even sleep for that matter. If I add into that a fast-food diet or one that is high in hot, spicy food, it would be no surprise to a holistic healer that I was getting migraines. However, if I knew I had a tendency to overheat, I might try to get more sleep, get plenty of water, reduce my stimulation load, and eat cooling foods that might be enough to compensate for my basic underlying weakness and keep me symptom-free.

To a holistic healer, looking at the whole person, no detail about past, present, or even future plans is too insignificant. Diet, religion, physical symptoms, mental state and moods, food cravings, sexual activities, view on how the world works, job, and home environment are all fair game for questioning.

Energy and Energy Work

When we are talking about "energy," particularly in regards to health and healing, there are a number of subtle distinctions that need to be made.

First of all, it is important to remember that all energy in the universe is really just one single unified field. There is no difference in the essential nature of the energy anywhere in the universe. The energy inside my body and the energy outside the body are the same energy. The energy that keeps the rocks on top of a mountain from tumbling down is the same as the energy in the wind and the caloric energy in the lunch I ate yesterday. We are truly One. However, energy can *appear* to be quite different depending on its location and actions. This can be useful because by allowing us to use descriptive words for the actions and location of energy, it gives us a way to conceptualize and work with that aspect of energy as a distinct unit. For example, electricity and gravity are both energy. Among other things, they share the common qualities of activating and making things move. They are both energy but it is easier for us to understand and work with them if we conceptualize them as different phenomena.

Where the problem arises, especially in healing work, is that sometimes our descriptors may unintentionally overlap. In the healing arts, energy when it is outside of the body is often called something different after it enters the body. In Chinese medicine there is talk about your "postnatal energy," which is all the energy you bring into your body through food, breathing, energy work, and so on. That same energy is then called different names depending on where it is and what it is doing. Your body's immune system is called your "defensive energy," whereas the energy that makes your digestive system excrete gastric juices and contract your stomach muscles is called your "stomach energy," and the energy that is being used by your body to repair injuries is called your "construction energy." They are all the same energy. It is just doing different things in different places. However, because they are all one, any change in one type of energy will affect the energy everywhere in your body, which in turn will affect how you live your life. For example, if your body is busy repairing after a surgery, it will generally make you more tired and in need of more rest. This will cut down on the number and intensity of the activities in which you can participate. This in turn will affect the people and events around you and so on across the unified field of energy. Nothing is an absolute. Everything is relative to the greater whole. So to truly be a holistic healer, one must have bifocal vision, looking at people and the world through one eye that sees everything as distinct parts, and the other eye that sees everything as fully connected.

Second, in general, energy has two primary activities:

Manifesting   Activating

Manifesting, which in Chinese medicine is called yin, is about contraction and solidification. By slowing down, contracting, and solidifying energy, the material universe is created. By contrast, activating, which in Chinese medicine is called yang, is about speeding up, moving, expanding, and dispersing energy. It is by moving, changing, and growing that life is created and maintained. Both are necessary for existence. In the world and the human body, if either force becomes too dominant, the result is death.

These two activities are continually in relationship. There are five forms that this relationship takes:

Opposition
Interdependence
Interconsuming and supporting
Intertransforming
Infinite divisibility

Opposition

The manifesting and activating activities serve as checks and balances on each other. The activating force keeps things from becoming stagnant, stale, and lifeless. The manifesting force keeps things from spinning out of control, breaking up, and dispersing into nothingness. In the body, the activating force is fire, heat, movement, upward and outward movement, excitement, and the energy that runs the various functions of the body, such as pumping the heart, expanding and contracting the lungs, and controlling all the other functions of the body. Too much activation, however, leads to extreme fevers, inflammations, manic episodes, high blood pressure, aneurisms, and other examples of too much heat, pressure, movement, and expansion. In the body, the manifesting force is water, cold, stillness, inhibition, downward and inward movement, and the nourishment and moistening of the basic building blocks of tissue construction and life. Too much manifesting, however, leads to extreme chills, water build up, phlegm, organs that stop functioning, depression, tumors and cancer, and other examples of too much inhibition and stagnation.

Interdependence

While manifesting and activating forces keep each other under control, they also need each other in order to exist. The activating force has no physical component, thus it needs the manifested material to carry it. On the contrary, the manifesting force has no force to make it move. An analogy that might help would be that of a car. The physical body of the car is the manifesting force. The actual movement of the car forward or backward is the activating force. The car (manifesting) cannot move unless something pushes it. However, the activating force cannot be generated without the manifested physical components of the gas, air, and combustion engine. In our bodies, the manifesting energy is the nutrient substances that our body uses to live and the activating energy is the functional activity of our organs. The functional activity (activating energy) of our digestive organs creates the nutritive substances (manifesting energy) that creates and maintains our digestive organs so that they can continue to function. A breakdown in either results in serious health problems.

Interconsuming and Supporting

Both manifesting and activating energies use up each other in the process of supporting one another. That is, when our organs are performing their function of creating nutrients, energy is used. In turn, some of these nutrients are then burned to create the energy the organs use in their functions. Therefore, the process of making manifesting energy burns activating energy that then has to burn manifesting energy to continue operating.

Intertransforming

Either manifesting or activating energy, taken to its extreme, will become its opposite. Once energy is all dispersed, it becomes stagnation. If stagnation and concentration persists too long, it eventually explodes. For example, a forest fire (excess activating energy) will burn up all the fuel and eventually die out (manifesting energy). By contrast, damp cold wet rags (manifesting energy) or grass often begin to molder and eventually burst into flames (activating energy). These same principles apply in the human body.

Infinite Divisibility

This is a reminder of the relative nature of manifesting and activating energies. Everything is a varying degree of both manifesting and activating. Up is activating and down is manifesting. So because of the general properties of these energies, my upper body is more activating and my lower body is more manifesting. However, my upper body can again be divided in two halves, and again and again, each being a relative relationship between manifesting and activating energies. Furthermore, the back of things is more activating, as is right sidedness. The front and left sides of things are more manifesting. Thus, while both my hands are more activating in relation to my feet, the back of my hand is more activating than the front, and the back of my right hand is the most activating of all of them. But even that can be infinitely divided into relative amounts of activating and manifesting energy.

Within the body these energies manifest as:

The vital life force
The essential substances of the body that maintains its vital
    activities

The vital life force, called Qi or Ki in Oriental medicine, is the energy on which you run. It permeates all parts of the body. If it is not present, there is death. This life force promotes the bodily functioning, growth, and development. It also warms, protects from external pathological influences, keeps water metabolism under control so that body fluids do not leak out, and controls the activities of the organs and tissues. If there is not sufficient life force in an organ or tissue, it will become cold and nonfunctioning. If an organ is deficient in vital life force, it will not perform effectively, which will, in turn, affect the other organs and ultimately the overall vital life force.

Blood and the nutrients it carries and body fluids make up the majority of the essential substances. They nourish and moisten the various tissues and organs of the body. Without sufficient essential substances, the muscles begins to atrophy, the joints stiffen, vision fades, the skin gets dry and irritated, and the body is slow to maintain and repair itself. Organs start to break down, which impairs their ability to generate vital life force and more essential substances.

The essential substances are created by our organs out of the nutrients and energy in the food and water we consume and the air we breathe. The vital life force is a combination of that spark of life we got from our parents during conception, the energy we get from the air we breathe, the food we eat, and the energy we take in from the world around us, consciously and unconsciously.

Pathogenesis

In the field of healing, almost all illness is considered to be due to a problem with the vital life force that in turn causes problems with the essential substances and organ functioning. Problems with the vital life force can be one of three types:

Excess
Deficiency
Blockage

An excess of vital life force is just that—too much energy concentrated somewhere. A deficiency of vital life force is too little energy in all or part of the body, and a blockage is a place where the energy is blocked and thus cannot flow freely from one place to another. In theory, you can never have too much vital life force. Therefore, almost all excesses of vital life force are due to a blockage somewhere that is causing a build up on one side of the blockage and a deficiency on the other side. Deficiencies can happen on their own with or without prior blockages. However, if a deficiency condition exists long enough, things will begin to stagnate and block up, which in turn may create an "upstream" excess. A good analogy for this is of a garden hose through which muddy water is traveling. As long as there is good water pressure, the muddy water will just flow through the hose. However, if the pressure is low so that the water just trickles through, over time it may leave dirt deposits that will build up and plug the hose. Once the hose is plugged, the water pressure may build up above the blockage while below it there would be no water at all.

Things that can affect the vital life energy are:

Genetics
Diet and lifestyle
Emotions
Injuries and bites
External pernicious influences

Genetics

As discussed earlier, everyone is born with certain genetic strengths and weaknesses. For example, some people are just born with weak lungs. From an energetic perspective, this lung weakness limits the amount of vital energy they would normally draw through breathing. This then means that they either have to increase their other sources of vital energy, for example, through diet or energy work, or live with an overall energy deficiency that will eventually impair functioning of their other organs. By contrast, they may have been born with a particularly stellar digestive strength that will provide the extra vital energy needed.

Diet and Lifestyle

Because a large amount of a person's vital life force comes from the food and water he or she consumes, diet can be a major factor in how much energy a person has and how it flows. In general, overeating uses up too much of the digestive system's energy. Over time, the digestive energy will become deficient, digestion will stagnate, and overall energy will drop. Eating too many cold or raw foods also weakens the digestive energy because it takes extra energy to heat up cold food or break down raw ones. Again, stagnation of food, water, and energy can result. However, too much consumption of hot, spicy food overfeeds the digestive fire, which can run rampant and cause inflammation or other hot conditions in the body, especially in the chest and head. Acid reflux, migraines, ringing in the ears, and red cheeks due to rosacea are not uncommon. Too much greasy foods or alcohol is the worst of both worlds. It causes digestive stagnation and congestion and is also overheating. There are other foods that have specific effects on the body's functioning and vital energy but they take years of study to master and are beyond the scope of this book.

Similarly, a person's lifestyle can either enhance or deplete his or her vital life force. "Burning the candle at both ends" consumes vital body energies at an accelerated rate. Overstrain through work or even too much exercise also uses up vital energies and can leave the body depleted. Excessive mental strain, stress, or overstimulation are also depleting. On the contrary, a lack of exercise, challenges to mind and body, or other types of stimulation will impair the circulation of vital life force through the body. As with exercise, to build and maintain muscle tone, resistance is needed. Without mental and physical resistance that forces you to exercise your mind and body, you lose your vital energy tone.

Emotions

In Oriental medicine, it is believed that emotions can have a major impact on one's health. In particular, there are three scenarios that have the highest likelihood of causing damage:

Long-term situations that elicit a strong emotion
Past emotions that someone holds onto for a long time
Random outbursts of emotion

Long-term exposure to situations that elicit strong emotions can cause injury to one's vital life force. These are usually situations where the emotion is the appropriate one for what is going on but it just goes on for too long. A child who grows up in an unsafe environment would eventually be affected by experiencing fear for too long. A person whose life and work is highly stressful and worrisome can also be adversely affected.

Similarly, holding onto past emotions for too long can also be injurious. These are situations where the emotion felt was appropriate for the life event but then is never let go of. Whether the emotion is grief over past losses, anger over past mistreatment, or fear over past environments, if the emotion and attendant energy of that emotion are not released, they will cause injury to the person's vital life force.

Lastly, we probably all know people who are sad when things are good or who get angry over the slightest things. If someone keeps experiencing an emotion when it is not situationally appropriate or frequently overreacts emotionally to minor situations, then he or she is already energetically imbalanced. As long as this person remains in this state, he or she will be affecting the vital life force of his or her entire body and over time this will begin to affect his or her general health.

Strong emotions affect the circulation of vital life force and essential substances in the body. In turn, this injures specific organs depending on the emotion.

Anger

Close your eyes and take a moment to relax. Now bring into your memory a situation that made you angry or imagine a situation that would make you very angry. Try to make the experience as real as possible. Notice how the anger feels in your body. What happens to your general energy level? What happens to your muscles?

You probably noticed that anger causes vital life force to rise up. Because of this, your head and upper body get warmer and your muscles get tense. You become more alert and energized because of the energy rushing to your head. The organ that is affected by anger is the liver.

Fear

Close your eyes again and take a moment to clear any previous feelings and sensations from your mind and body. Now bring into your memory or imagination a situation in which you feel fearful. It can be fearful for your own or someone else's safety and security. Try to make the experience as real as possible. How does fear feel in your body? What happens this time to your general energy level?

In this case, you probably felt your energy level move to the lower part of your body. Fear causes vital life force to decline to your abdomen and legs. According to Chinese medicine, the core of your vital life force is in your kidneys. When your life is threatened, your energy moves back to your core to protect your vital organs and keep it ready for distribution as needed for either fight or flight. In many cases, you may notice that the decline of energy includes your legs, which are being readied for rapid flight if necessary. The organs affected by long-term or excessive fear are your kidneys and adrenal glands.

Grief

As before, close your eyes and clear away any previous feelings and sensations. Bring into your memory or imagination a situation

that causes you extreme sadness and grief. Most of us have experi-
enced at least one major loss that is still a little sore. Bring your grief
and sadness back into full awareness. How does your grief feel in
your body? Where do you feel your grief? What does grief do to your
general energy level?

Ever notice that after a long period of crying you feel completely wiped out of energy? Ever fall asleep crying? That is because grief and sadness consume your vital life energy. In this
exercise you probably noticed that you felt heavy but unlike feeling anger or fear, not energized in any particular way. No fight or
flight mechanism was energized or triggered. You may also have
noticed that the heaviness centered on your chest. Your lungs are
the organs injured by excessive sadness and grief. And because
your lungs are one of the major sources of new vital life force in
your body, if they become injured due to an extended period of
grief, they become less able to bring in new energy and thus your
general energy level begins to drop.

Worry

Close your eyes and again clear away any previous feelings and
sensations. Now bring into your memory or imagination a situation
that causes you to worry. Because of our stress-laden society, you
probably won't have any problem finding something. Focus on that
stressor. Notice how your general energy level and body respond to
your worry.

Excessive worry causes your vital life force to stagnate. Just
as your mind enters into a loop where you keep going over and
over the same situation, so your vital life force gets trapped and
fails to circulate effectively. For that reason, you probably noticed that your energy tended to focus in your head. Otherwise,
you probably didn't feel overly energetic or motivated to move or

do anything. Over time, if someone is constantly stressed and worried, the lack of circulation of energy and essential substances throughout the body will begin to deprive the other organs and tissues. In turn, they will begin to work less effectively and various chronic degenerative symptoms will begin to show up. The organs injured by excessive worry are the stomach and spleen.

Overstimulation

Close your eyes and clear away any previous lingering feelings and sensations. Take a few moments to remember or imagine a time when you were so excited and stimulated that you could barely contain yourself. Remember how you felt after you had been in this state for a while. After the initial rush, what happened to your energy level after the overstimulation kicked in? What happened in your body?

Overstimulation, or excessive joy as the Chinese call it, causes your vital life force to slow down. Initially, there is that rush of energy and excitement, but after a while you probably noticed that you just gradually slowed to almost a stop. It is like the sensation you get after playing a video game for eight hours straight. You aren't really tired but you can't seem to get yourself to do anything else besides play video games. So you just sit there without much thought or motivation. Overstimulation injures your heart, slows your mind, and dulls your spirit. In general, our culture is highly overstimulated.

Injuries and Bites

Another area of potential adverse affect to vital life energy is through actual bites and injuries. Injuries that cause bruising and breaking disturb the free flow of vital life energy and cause blockages. Cuts, punctures, and other sources of bleeding cause a loss of blood and the energy that flows with it. Furthermore, as soon as an injury happens, the body immediately starts to divert energy to the injured area and those organs specifically involved in tissue repair. That diversion will cause general energy deficiencies throughout the rest of the body and explains why we need to sleep so much when we are healing. Our body doesn't have enough energy to both repair itself and go about our regular business. Once repair is done, scar tissue can often be a source of chronic or reoccurring blockages of energy.

External Pernicious Influences

There are five environmental conditions that can influence your vital life energy and essential substances. They are called "external" because they are influences that come from outside of the body. They are called "pernicious" because they are harmful to the body. The five influences are: cold, heat, dryness, dampness, and wind.

Although they are considered to be the causative factors in several kinds of conditions, at this level of training and practice the real value in knowing them is because their symptoms are very descriptive of similar conditions. That is, a hot condition in the body, regardless of whether it came from internal or external sources, will still show the same signs. As nonprofessional healers, you don't need to distinguish whether the heat in the body came from an outside source or an inside source, only that there is heat in the body. So by learning the signs of each external influence, you are also learning the signs that would be present due to a similar internal influence. Treatments at this level of practice will be the same regardless of where the heat came from.

Cold

Picture in your mind a block of ice surrounded by snow. Notice the clearness of the ice and the white of the snow. The ice feels cold and dry. Notice how cold makes everything contract with the exception of water, which expands when it freezes.

Cold in the body is recognizable by all these signs. If a body part feels cold and is white, it is being affected by cold. Because cold contracts things, it tends to cause stagnation and pain. This includes tight, sore muscles and stomach cramps. The stagnation can cause blood to stagnate, which can lead to a bluish-white color. Also, because fluids stagnate, the body stops sweating and the eyes and skin can become dry. On the flip side, because water expands when frozen, cold can cause copious clear nasal discharge, increased flow of clear urine, and watery diarrhea.

Heat

Picture in your mind a fire. Notice the bright reds and yellows of the flame, the black of the charred wood, and the gray of the ashes. Feel the hot dryness of the fire. Notice how the flame rises upward and dances about restlessly.

These are all symptoms of heat in the body. Anytime you see red or yellow in the body, it is heat of some sort. If you see black or gray, this is probably a sign of extreme consumption of bodily fluids due to heat. The fire is literally burning up the body. Skin that feels hot to the touch and any kind of inflammation in the body is also heat. Heat causes sweating and dries out the body. Heat tends to rise upward, so hot symptoms are more likely in the upper part of the body. These can include red eyes, pressure or heat in the head, ringing in the ears, and headaches. In the digestive system, heat can present as a burning, acidic feeling in the stomach, acid reflux, gas, and vomiting. If heat is in the lower body, it can show up as yellow urine and explosive diarrhea. Because of the heat's tendency to rise, when it disturbs your mind it causes irritability and restlessness.

Dryness

Although dryness can be caused by heat, cold, and even wind, it can also exist simply by itself. In the body it can cause chapped lips, dry skin, thirst, a dry cough, reduced urination, and constipation.

Dampness

Imagine a sticky, stinky swamp. Notice how everything gets bogged down and heavy. Dampness in the body does the same thing. It tends to make things feel heavy and slows down one's digestion and elimination. You get mucus in your nose, mouth, and throat and oozing, foul smelling discharges. Dampness can be, and usually is, combined with either hot or cold symptoms.

Wind

Imagine a tree on a windy day. Picture how the wind makes the branches sway back and forth, never holding still. See how the wind makes leaves on the ground blow up into the air before settling back down again. Feel the drying effect of the wind. In very high winds, notice how the wind pins things down so that they cannot move at all.

Pathogenic wind in the body shows up as pain and other symptoms that come and go or move from place to place. Like the wind, they come on quickly. Because wind tends to disperse energy upward and outwardly like leaves, it usually affects the upper part of the body and the extremities. Head, neck, face, and limbs are often affected. When affecting the mind, wind causes dizziness, vertigo, and convulsion. In extreme cases, it can cause paralysis such as is found in Bell's palsy.

Wind is almost always seen in conjunction with heat, cold, dryness, or dampness. It seldom appears alone. As an external factor, wind is necessary to bring the other pernicious influences into the body. Conversely, heat, cold, dryness, and dampness can each cause wind in the body.

This concludes the basic concepts and definitions. It may seem like a lot to remember, but keep in mind that everything in natural healing is metaphorical. Each of these concepts is based on phenomena seen in nature, which makes it particularly well suited to Wiccan healers. By taking time to fully grasp these core concepts, you will be amazed at how much easier it is to diagnosis the nature of a condition and to come up with a customized magickal treatment for it.

Diagnosis

Before trying to magically or energetically heal someone, it is important to know the nature of the problem and where it is located in the body. At a professional level where you are performing physical treatments and prescribing herbs to ingest, this can get very complicated. For magickal and energetic healers, the process is much simpler. You are trying to answer these four questions:

1. Is this a deficiency, an excess, or a blockage?
2. Is this a hot, cold, or neutral condition?
3. Is there dryness or dampness present?
4. Where are the symptoms showing up?

To answer these questions, there are five types of diagnostic methods: seeing, listening, smelling, asking, and touching.

Seeing

Take a moment to stand in front of a mirror. A full-length mirror is best. Just gaze into the mirror at your reflection. Do not focus on any particular body part. Do not judge or criticize. Just take in the image as if it were a painting or sculpture. Notice how lively or dull the image looks. Does it look vital or run-down? If you can see auras, look at the image's aura. Are there any dull patches or holes in the aura? Look at the color of the image's complexion. Is it pale or pink? Are there any patches of other colors on the face and body? Notice the basic symmetry of the body. Are there any places that are not symmetrical? Is one shoulder slightly higher than the other? Is the image standing on one leg, shifting its hips, spine, and shoulder to one side? Is one side of the body better developed? How about top versus bottom? Is the image larger on bottom than top or vice versa? Or is it larger in the middle and smaller on the extremities? Again, do not judge. Just take note. Lastly, stick out your tongue as far as you can. Take note of the texture and color of the various parts of your tongue. Is there a coating on the tongue? If so, what color and how thick is it?

Vitality

This is an indicator of a general level of vital life force. Vitality is judged by looking at a person's eyes when he or she walks into the room. Do they sparkle? Do they look lively and engaged or are they kind of dull and poorly focused? A person cannot have too much vitality, nor will a blockage show up through this method; however, if vitality is low, you can be certain that this is a deficiency condition of some sort.

Auras

These can serve a wide variety of diagnostic purposes; however, it can take many years of study to become truly proficient in reading auras. Still, even beginning healers can use them effectively to diagnose the general energy level of a person and where specific deficiencies, excesses, and blockages may reside. Regardless of color, a bright, vibrant aura indicates sufficient energy. A dull aura indicates a deficiency. Furthermore, if any holes can be seen in the aura, they indicate places that are deficient in energy. Conversely, excessively bright spots in the aura can indicate places of excess energy, probably due to blockage.

Color

The color, especially of the face, indicates the presence of heat, cold, dampness, deficiency, and/or blockage. Anything that is red is showing heat signs. Yellow indicates heat with the addition of dampness. Anything that is white, and any fluids that are copious and clear, indicate cold. A pale complexion indicates a deficiency of blood. There just isn't enough blood in the skin to make it pink. By contrast, blue indicates stagnation of blood due to a blockage. Gray indicates extreme deficiency after heat has burned up all the resources.

Body

The symmetry, or lack thereof, of a person's body can be used to locate where energy is blocked and areas of relative excess and deficiency. If there is a blockage, the excess energy will make that area tight and possibly in spasm. That will cause the person to hold him- or herself in an uneven manner. If the condition persists long enough, it may even overdevelop some part of his or her body in comparison to the rest. This typically develops into an excess on one side of the body and a deficiency on the other.

Tongue

Tongue diagnosis is a very complex method of diagnosis in Chinese medicine. However, some of the basics can be used quite effectively for magickal healers to pinpoint the problem.

In tongue diagnosis you look at both the body of the tongue and the coating on the tongue. The coating indicates the presence of heat, cold, dryness, or dampness, especially in the digestive tract. The tongue should have a very thin white coating over the entire body of the tongue. If there is no coating, then a dryness condition exists. If a thick coating is present, then there is dampness. If the thick coating is white, then the problem is a cold one. If the coating is yellow, then there is dampness and heat.

The body of the tongue indicates how well blood, fluids, and vital life energy are circulating in the body. It should be pink and meaty. If the tongue is pale, then there is a deficiency of blood in the body. If the tongue is also very thin, it indicates that the blood deficiency has been going on for a long time. If the tongue is purple, there is stagnation of blood. If the tip of the tongue is red, then there is heat in the person's body. If the whole tongue is red, the heat is very strong. If the sides of the tongue have teeth marks in them, then the vital life energy is deficient.

Listening

When we listen diagnostically, we are listening to two things: the person's speech and breathing. How we speak generally indicates how much energy we have. A feeble, low voice indicates a deficiency of energy. A lusty voice or one that is overly loud or dramatic indicates an excess of energy. Feeble breathing and/or a weak cough indicate a person who is deficient in energy. Forceful, coarse breathing or a cough indicates a condition that is excess in nature.

Smelling

For the most part, if someone has a strong body smell, then he or she has an excess condition. If the smell is of body sweat, then he or she has a heat excess. If the body smell is sour, then he or she has a blockage in the digestive system.

Asking

Next ask the patient to describe his or her condition. You want to get as much information as possible. You are looking to discover if the problem is excess, deficiency, or blockage and whether there are heat, cold, dampness, dryness, or wind symptoms. If the illness is chronic, you are likely to find that the person has a few of each. You also want to know exactly where the problem is.

Touching

There are three main ways in which touching can be used diagnostically:

Feeling the energy pathways
Body palpation
Pulse taking

Feeling the Energy Pathways

In this type of touching, you don't actually touch the physical body at all. Clear your mind. Decide which hand you feel more receptive in. For most people it is their left hands but not always. Hold your receptive hand, palm down, about two inches off the person's body. Slowly scan the body for problem spots. You should feel a steady amount of energy in the form of pressure and heat coming off the person's body. If as you scan you find places that feel hot or cold, note them. Similarly, if you notice the pressure on your palm drop or rise dramatically, then you have found spots of deficient energy and excess energy, respectively. Again, note where and what you find.

Body Palpation

Palpation is actually feeling around to find the sore spots. The person can usually put you in the general location, or you may have found them through your energy scan, but then you need to feel around to find exactly where and how it hurts. You should also press around in the surrounding area. Many times pain is "referred" from another spot. That is, it hurts worse somewhere other than where the actual problem is. For example, many people with neck problems experience shoulder pain. It is often the shoulder pain they come in for, but by pressing around, you can find that the neck is also sore. By treating both the local pain area and the source area you can get better results than simply treating the symptomatic area.

Once you have located the sore spots, notice if they feel better or worse when you put pressure on them. If they feel better, then they are deficient and need more energy. If adding energy in the form of pressure hurts more, then they have a blockage and excess. Ideally, these should confirm your findings from the body energy scan. If they contradict one another, then you need to look further into what is going on.

Pulse Taking

There is a saying in Chinese medicine that it takes fifteen years of sustained practice at pulse taking to become barely adequate at it. After thirty years you are considered to have begun mastering the art. Obviously, this means that there is more to teach about pulse taking than can be covered in this chapter. However, there are some general qualities of the pulse that even a beginner can pick up and use.

Place the middle finger of your right hand on the radial pulse in your left wrist. You can find this pulse by holding your left arm palm up and tracing from your thumb to just above your wrist. You should find a bony bump there that is your radial protuberance. Just beside that protuberance you will find your radial pulse. Begin by seeing how lightly or deeply you have to press to feel your pulse. How deep is your pulse? Next, notice how strong your pulse feels. Does it feel like the pounding surf, a small trickle, or something in between? Next, count how many beats your pulse makes for every cycle of breath you take. How many beats happen in the time it takes you to make one full inhale and exhale?

Now do the same thing for the pulse on your right wrist. Notice if any of your findings are different from the left to right wrist. Is one pulse stronger than the other? Deeper? Faster? Try this exercise on other people. How do their pulses differ from your pulse?

A normal, healthy pulse should be the same on both the left and right wrists. It should beat four to five times per each breath cycle. It should be neither too deep nor too shallow, nor too strong or too weak. Almost no one ever has a perfect pulse so do not panic if yours isn't perfect.

A pulse that differs from side to side shows a basic imbalance. One side of you is working harder than the other, which, over time will cause problems. A weak pulse that either has little pressure or feels like just a tiny string indicates deficiency. A pounding or hard, wiry pulse indicates an excess condition. A pulse that is faster than five beats per breath cycle is rapid and indicates heat. A pulse slower than four beats per breath cycle is slow and indicates cold. A pulse that you can feel right at the surface of the skin is a floating pulse and also indicates heat. A pulse that is deep indicates a cold condition. Most commonly, you will find the pulses in combinations such as a rapid, floating pulse or a slow, deep pulse.

Putting It All Together

Once you have gathered all this diagnostic data, whether on yourself or someone else, the next step is to put it all together and come to some conclusions. You almost certainly have more information than you really need, but remember that holistic healers see the body as a whole package where each part influences and reflects the health of the other parts. So if you overlook one piece of information, you may actually miss a critical clue as to the problem. However, in reality, you probably got a wide spectrum of seemingly conflicting data. Parts of the person may be hot and others cold. They may have lung dryness and stomach dampness. They may seem deficient in general energy but have muscular blockages and excesses of energy.

Remember, you are trying to answer these four questions:

1. Is this a deficiency, an excess, or a blockage?
2. Is this a hot, cold, or neutral condition?
3. Is there dryness or dampness present?
4. Where are the symptoms showing up?

At this point, you should be able to tell from the person's vitality, aura, and pulses whether his or her general overall energy is normal or deficient. From your scans, palpations, and questions, you should be able to identify the specific locations of problems and if they are deficient, excess, hot, or cold. Lastly, from pulse and tongue diagnosis you should be able to tell if any heat or cold problems are deep-seated or just superficial. If they are deep-seated, they will show up in the pulses and tongue. If they are just superficial, localized problems, they will not show up.

So now you can answer these additional questions:

1. Is there an overall energy deficiency?
2. Is there a deep-seated heat or cold condition?

If neither of these two is "yes," then the problem is superficial and all your treatments can be directed locally. If either or both is a "yes," then they need to be addressed before or concurrently with the rest of the problems.

Treatment

Treatment Strategies and Rationales

The strategies for healing are very straightforward once a diagnostic assessment has been done. Deficiencies are fixed by adding what is missing. Removing blockages and draining energy out treats excesses. Heat is treated with cold, and cold is treated with heat. Dampness needs to be dried out and dryness needs moisture added.

If a person has an underlying condition of vital energy or blood deficiency, then these need to be addressed before any long-term healing can take place. You can try to provide temporary relief of the symptoms, but the body will have trouble really healing if it does not have the resources to do so. Similarly, if an underlying heat condition exists, any treatment to cool localized inflammations will only be temporary. Without addressing the underlying heat, the condition will keep coming back. The same scenario exists for underlying cold conditions as well.

Once the underlying problems are taken care of, the body will usually heal itself without any other assistance. If not, localized treatments based entirely on the particular conditions of each should be effective.

Raising and Applying Energy Work Specifically for Diagnosis

As stated earlier, energy work includes every kind of raising, channeling, focusing, and moving of energy. In the realm of healing, energy work can involve meditations, raising and projecting energy, rituals, spells, and the application of magickal stones and herbs. The following is an example of some of the types of energy healing work that can be used for the various specific types of problems and the rationale behind choosing that type of energy work. Each of these conditions could also benefit from changes in diet and lifestyle that would compliment the energy work.

General Energy Deficiency

If the person has an underlying energy deficiency, then the first thing that needs to be done is to restore his or her level of energy. Spells and rituals that raise energy and then put it into the body of the person would be very beneficial. Another approach is for the person to do a daily energy exercise him- or herself. Qi Gong, which literally means "energy breath work," is particularly useful.

Meditation: Bringing in the Energy of Nature Qi Gong

All exhaling and inhaling are done through your nose. Stand with your feet shoulder width apart. Place one hand with your palm touch-

ing just below your navel. Place the other hand on top of the first hand. Exhale fully and as you begin to inhale, link your fingers together and slowly bring your hands up your body.

At your chest level, turn your palms away from your body and keep extending your arms until your arms are stretched fully upward, your fingers still linked, your palms pointed toward the sky. You should time your inhalation so it ends just as your arms reach full extension. As you do this, imagine that you are bringing the energy of the earth up through your body and connecting it with the energy of the sky.

As you begin to exhale, separate your fingers and bring your arms down toward your sides, palms facing away from your body. Stop when your arms are level with your shoulders, straight out to each side so that you form a T. As you exhale, imagine that you are pushing out through your palms any unhealthy or negative energy.

As you begin to inhale again, imagine that your hands are giant scoops. Move your arms in a scooping motion so that you are scooping energy back to the spot underneath your navel. At the end of your inhalation, your hands should be back to where you began, overlapped just below your navel. Exhale again and as you do so, imagine pushing all the energy that you scooped up with your hands into your body at that spot below your navel.

Repeat the process at least ten times. When you are done, rub your palms vigorously together for a few seconds and then run them over your eyes, ears, nose, and mouth, down your body and back to below your navel.

General Blood Deficiency

As with energy deficiency, a general blood deficiency must be addressed before any other problems. As one of the essential substances, blood is responsible for nourishing the tissues. It is primarily manifesting in nature and without sufficient amounts of blood the body cannot heal. There are several ways in which this can be accomplished. One way is to give energy specifically to those organs associated with blood manufacture. Then, provided the person eats a healthy diet, the body should take care of itself.

Spellworking: Digestive Energy

Everyone in the ritual should ground and center. Take a moment for everyone to focus their intention on bringing in energy that will be neither hot nor cold, but that will assist the production and distribution of blood and nutrients in the body. Cast a ritual space appropriate for raising and focusing energy. Begin to raise magickal energy. Perhaps some people could drum, others dance, and still others chant. As the energy rises, people should focus on sending their energy to the healer. The healer places his or her hands on the person's abdomen and focuses his or her intent to give energy to the stomach, liver, and spleen. The group can continue to raise and send energy to the person through the healer until the healer feels like the work is complete. Everyone should ground any excess energy and uncast the ritual space. This ritual can also be done at a distance with the healer imagining putting his or her hands over the person's abdomen.

Underlying Heat

If someone has a deep, internal heat problem, he or she probably has a variety of heat symptoms in various systems of the body manifesting as inflammation. The general strategy is to surround and fill him or her with cooling water to put out the inner pathogenic fire.

Drawing Energy: Dowsing the Inner Fire

If possible, find a spot where you can sit or stand next to a body of water. A nice big bathtub will do in a pinch. Ground and center your mind and body. Immerse part or all of yourself in the water. Even just sticking your finger in the water will serve. As the water surrounds you, visualize your pores opening up and allowing the water to flow freely into and throughout your body. Feel the water coursing through your veins, between your tissues and organs, and into every little cell of your body. Feel the cooling, calming, and healing effects of the water. Visualize it putting out any hot, inflamed areas, leaving them cool, relaxed, and rejuvenated. When you feel ready, open your eyes and get out of the water. Thank the water for removing your pain.

Underlying Cold

As with internal heat, if someone has a deep, internal cold problem, the cold is probably affecting several of his or her body's systems. In this case, the general strategy is to surround and fill them with something that will warm them up. Besides all the previous techniques that would work, invocation of warming solar energy is also an option to bring in healing heat.

Invocation: Filled with the Sun

Find a warm, comfortable place in the sun. Close your eyes, relax, and ground and center. Quiet your mind and body. When you are quiet, direct your focus to the sun above you and the sunlight as it bathes your body. Raise your arms toward the sun, palms open and up. In your mind, send out a call asking the sun to descend into your body. In your imagination, see the sun literally descending, slowly coming down out of the sky and entering your body. Feel the heat and light center in your heart. Feel the light beaming through every cell of your body, carrying warmth and health throughout. After you have bathed in the sun for several minutes, thank the sun for coming into you and bid it farewell. Imagine the sun slowly rising back out of your body, up into the sky to its rightful place.

Localized Blockage: Excess and Deficiency

A common mistake made by beginning healers is the assumption that every problem can be helped just by adding healing energy. However, that is not necessarily the case when it comes to blockages. Blockages are usually in the muscle or joints and cause swelling and inflammation. They are frequently caused by tension or physical injury that blocks the free flow of vital energy. If there is a blockage, just adding energy to it will further compact the blockage, add to the excess, and cause more pain. First, the excess energy already present needs to be drained. Second, energy must be passed *through* and not just added. The movement of energy through the area will break up the blockage. There are many ways to accomplish this. Here is one using your hands.

Moving Blockages

Find where the blockage is. Palpate around the area until you know exactly where the blockage begins and ends, which side of it has excess energy, and which side has deficient energy. With your fingers, massage the area starting in the excess area and moving toward the deficient area. You may also want to take a quartz crystal and put the base of it on the excess area, drawing the energy up into the crystal. Then take the crystal and put its point to the deficient area, allowing the energy to drain from the crystal. Do this as long as it takes. It may even require several sessions.

After the excess is drained, take your projective hand and place it on one side of the blockage. Place your receptive hand on the other side of the blockage. Send energy from one hand to the other, just skimming through the top layers of the body. You want to make sure that you take back in all the energy you send out. The goal is not to add energy but to wear away the blockage. When you feel like your energy passes through with less resistance, move your hands to a different angle around the blockage and again pass energy through the area. Continue this process until you no longer feel a blockage.

Localized Heat or Cold

Occasionally, we take on localized areas of heat or cold. Muscle strain will leave a muscle inflamed. Sitting for long periods may slow circulation enough to allow cold to get into a joint, making it stiff and sore. Neither of these superficial, localized conditions requires major systemic intervention. In fact, to do a generalized heating or cooling ritual might actually fix the localized problem but cause a more serious, deeper problem. For this kind of problem, the goal is simply to add heat or cold, both physically and energetically, to the area.

Healing with Stones

Locate the precise area that needs to be heated or cooled. Begin by actually physically heating or cooling the area. Hot packs, heated towels, or even heat lamps can be used to warm the area if it is cold. Conversely, ice packs work well to reduce localized inflammation. After physically changing the temperature, place a healing stone on the area. Aquamarine, azurite, and jade are cooling, whereas carnelian, garnet, and rhodocrosite are heating stones. Leave the stone on the spot for a half hour and then finish up with physically heating or cooling the area again.

Energy work in general and healing work specifically is a multifaceted process. In many cases, any attempt to sending healing or other magickal energy is usually better than none. However, Oriental medicine has always taught that it is better to administer an inferior treatment to the right place than to administer a strong, superior treatment to the wrong place. Adept healers have the ability to both correctly diagnosis the problem and to effectively treat it.

Once you have mastered the ability to heal yourself and others, you are ready to move onto the next step in the circle of knowledge. Through healing you have made yourself and others whole. Now you will learn how to transform those whole selves into higher levels of spiritual development.

CHAPTER 6

Progress by Degrees: Models and Methods of Initiation

Many Wiccan and other magickal groups use initiations for their members. What many beginning and intermediate practitioners do not realize is that various initiatic groups use these rituals in very different ways and for different purposes. They can be used as transformative ritual, learning experiences, and/or ceremonies to mark spiritual achievement and growth. Many groups use initiations as varying degrees of all these. But even then, what precisely is begun? What are the mechanisms for kicking off the process? What about later initiations? Are they beginnings, progress reports, or graduations? As a Wiccan adept attuned to the forces of nature and the will of the Divine, you are a powerful tool for transformation and change in the world. In that role, you will frequently find yourself with the responsibility of facilitating growth and change in yourself and others. Therefore, it is your duty to know precisely how initiations work and how to apply them for maximal transformation.

Definitions

To begin with, let's clarify our terms.

The word "initiation" comes from the Latin *initi(um)* which

159

literally means "beginning." Therefore, at its most general meaning, "initiation" simply refers to commencing a new endeavor.
More specifically, however, the dictionary defines "initiation" as
the introduction into the secret knowledge of some art or subject,
and/or the formal admission into a society, club, or group that
keeps such knowledge.

"Dedication" is defined as the act of setting apart and consecrating some thing or person to a deity or sacred purpose. It also
means the act of devoting oneself wholly and earnestly to some
person, cause, or purpose. In Wiccan practice, this type of ritual
marks the commitment of the person to a particular spiritual tradition, training program, or deity. Usually, dedications are for
a specific period of time, with one year and one day being traditional.

Dedications

Dedications are usually the first step in one's spiritual journey.
A dedication ritual is one where the dedicant is making a vow to
devote him- or herself wholly and earnestly to the sacred purpose
of the spiritual practice of Wicca.

If the dedicant is working solo, he or she will generally be ded-
icating him- or herself to the general study and practice of Wicca,
without reference to one or another group or tradition. If he or
she will be studying under a group, then his or her dedication may
also include a commitment to studying a particular style or tradition of Wicca with this particular group for a set period of time,
again, with one year and one day being usual. The dedicant is not
actually joining the group at this time, nor is the group offering
eventual membership. The dedication is simply an agreement to
put in the time and effort to see if this is the right path for the person to follow and whether or not the person and the group are a
good fit.

A Self-Dedication

You will need the following items:

A white candle

A bowl of water

Incense and holder

A lighter or matches to light the candle and incense

A small vial of anointing oil

3 strands of white cord, each long enough to go around your waist 3 times and touch the floor

5 beads of any color or style large enough to fit one strand of white cord

Any other ritual tools you may desire

A small altar table on which to put your tools

A copy of this ritual

Find a quiet, private, secure location where you will not be disturbed during the ritual. Remember to turn off all your phones and lock your doors if you have roommates. The ritual is best performed naked as a sign of newness and rebirth; however, it is not critical. Set up the altar and place the listed items on it. Light the incense, but do not light the candle yet. Take a moment to ground and center. Begin by casting a protective circle as described in chapter 2. Once the circle is complete, begin the ritual as follows:

Go to the altar and kneeling before it say:

Today, I begin a new life. I begin a journey down a new path of self-exploration and growth. I ask that the Powers of Nature be with me and guide me.

Pick up the bowl of water and say:

With this water, receptive and cleansing, I purify my body, mind, spirit, and soul so that I might be new again as I venture on my new path.

Put the bowl back onto the altar and dip your hands in the water. Rub water over your entire body, envisioning it being cleansed and purified.

When you are done, pick up the incense and say:

With this incense, active and blessing, I consecrate my body, mind, spirit, and soul so that I might be a worthy vessel for the knowledge and wisdom that I will receive.

Wave the incense around your body so that the smoke covers and blesses you. Return the incense to the altar.

Close your eyes and quiet your mind of any concerns. Breathe for a few moments and feel the magick swirling around you.

Open your eyes and say:

I dedicate myself to the God and Goddess; to honor and worship them. I pledge to diligently study and practice the path of Wicca, respecting that which I learn and keeping silent about my studies lest I dilute the solemnity of my pledge. I dedicate [insert a time period here — could be anywhere from a year and a day to your entire lifetime] to the service of the Old Gods. In dedication to them, I say:

With the oil, anoint yourself on your feet saying:

Blessed be my feet that will lead me on my path.

Anoint yourself on your knees saying:

Blessed be my knees that will kneel at the altars of the God and Goddess.

Anoint yourself on your genitals saying:

Blessed be my loins from which the creativity of the universe will flow.

Anoint yourself on your breast saying:

Blessed be my breasts that my heart may open up to the inspiration of the Divine.

Anoint yourself on your mouth saying:

Blessed be my lips that will learn to speak the sacred rites.

So mote it be.

After the final proclamation of dedication, light the white candle as a symbol of the new light or knowledge that you are bringing into your life.

The final piece of magick in this ritual is the making of your dedication cord. Take the three strands of white cord and tie them together at one end. Take the knot created and tuck it between two toes on your foot. Begin to braid the cords together, focusing entirely on putting your desire to learn and practice Wicca into each braid. Periodically, whenever your intuition tells you, put one of the beads onto one of the strands. These beads represent the five energy centers that you anointed: your feet, knees, loins, breasts, and lips. You are literally tying your stated intention to use these centers into the cord. Continue braiding, adding beads as your intuition dictates, until you have braided the entire cord. Tie the cord off at the end. This cord is your first ritual tool and should be worn during all study, ritual, and magickal practice during your time as a dedicant.

A group dedication would be very similar to this self-dedication except that it would use symbols, words, oaths, and maybe even God and Goddess names specific to its tradition. It would also probably include a dedication to study with the group for at least a year and a day, not to study with any other groups during that time, and not to reveal anything learned or the identities of any of the group members to anyone not in the group.

After a year and a day as a dedicant, it is time for you to decide about pursuing Wicca further. If after your studies you decide that Wicca is not for you, then you can simply thank the Gods for allowing you to learn of them and then begin a new path, or you may decide to take the next step in formal Wicca studies: initiation.

Initiations: Self vs. Group

There are many different types and styles of initiation. The very first differentiation is self-initiation versus group initiation.

Self-initiations are just that, initiations done to yourself by yourself. People choose self-initiations for a variety of reasons. One of the primary reasons is that there is no suitable local group in which to initiate. Either the practitioner lives in a region where there are not any Wiccan circles that are accepting new people, or for whatever reason, the person already knows that the local group will not be a good fit for him or her.

However, that is not the sole reason for choosing a self-initiation. Sometimes a person chooses to work as a solitary even if there are dozens of good covens in the area. For that person, the Goddess speaks in unique ways, urging the relinquishment of existing ritual forms, beliefs, and practices and the development of a personalized style. Therefore, the person chooses self-initiation as a way to initiate him- or herself into an individual relationship with the Gods without reference to other groups or traditions.

Lastly, even a person who is a member of an existing group, and perhaps has even been through a group initiation, may choose to go through a single or series of self-initiations, either to recognize growth and changes that have happened in his or her life— essentially, rite of passage rituals—or to stimulate new growth and changes. These transformational self-initiations would be custom designed to elicit specific changes that may be outside of the usual practices of most Wiccan groups. For example, I might want to do a series of ten personal challenges and ritual trials specifically around overcoming some childhood trauma. My coven might operate very formally, with specific curricula and ritual cycles that do not allow much room for extra work. In fact, if all thirteen members of my coven wanted a customized series of ten rituals, we'd have 130 rituals to do and no time for anything else! So for such situations, I might choose to design and perform my own self-initiations, perhaps with guidance and support from interested friends, elders, and coven mates.

Therefore, the three greatest benefits of self-initiations over group initiations are:

- They can be done with or without a group
- They can be customized to specific individual needs
- They can go deeper into individual personal transformation

Group initiations are, simply, initiations performed by a group. Group initiations can be performed on an individual, a small subset of the group, or the entire group on itself. The latter would, technically, be a group self-initiation.

The greatest benefits of group initiations over self-initiations are:

- A group can raise a greater amount of energy, thus making the entire ritual experience more powerful
- An established group potentially has more collective knowledge and wisdom to draw on
- A group can put on more elaborate rituals with varying characters, smoother prop movement, and better general collective preparation such as nicer props and gear
- The individual or individuals being initiated, unless this is a group self-initiation, are unaware of what to expect, thus

putting them into a heightened sense of awareness and the
potential for greater spiritual impact

Group initiations performed on individuals are by far the most
common in Wicca. Occasionally, when there are a large number
of initiates and a limited number of times a group can all meet, a
group might perform a group initiation on several new candidates at once. However, if done at all, it is more commonly done
for dedication than initiations and if done for initiations, is almost
always only done on the lowest, least advanced initiations. Group
self-initiations, being a hybrid of group and self-initiations, get the
benefits and limitations of both. They can be more readily customized for the group as a whole, raise more energy, and be more elaborate, but they still lack the depth of the individual self-initiation
and lose the mystery of not knowing the ritual beforehand.

Lastly, self-initiations of either individuals or groups lose the
benefits of the often-powerful elements of tradition and group-
mind that long established groups gain. Those elements, however, can also become limitations and dysfunction in unhealthy
groups. Group dynamics, internal politics between personalities,
scheduling challenges, and rigid uniformity are all areas of potential pitfall in groups. Therefore, remember that a good group can
be an indescribably powerful asset to one's personal and spiritual
growth, but a bad group can be downright damaging. Thus, as in
all things relating to Wicca, it is important to find which things
work and do not work for you, and if dealing with groups, always
maintain good ethics and personal boundaries, go into them with
your eyes open, and if your intuition tells you that things aren't
quite right, listen to it.

Many Wiccan and other magickal groups use initiations for
their members. Typically, after the dedication period of a year and
a day, when the student has learned all the basic information
and both he or she and the coven have decided that they are a
good fit together, the dedicant will be invited to be initiated into

the group. Then, as he or she progresses in learning and skill or to promote such progress, he or she will undergo subsequent initiations until he or she has mastered the tradition.

Initiations: Achievement vs. Transformation

A second differentiation in type and style of initiation revolves around the use of achievement recognition versus transformation promotion. The first gives recognition for progress made while the latter is designed to stimulate radical change.

Achievement ceremonies, like high school graduations, mark the attainment of a particular level of training, personal growth, and spiritual attainment. These rituals usually involve the granting of a title (e.g., priestess and witch) and perhaps conveyance of specialized information available only to those of that particular degree. So for example, in a common Wiccan initiation, once the initiate has studied for a certain length of time and passed the challenges of the degree, he or she is taught the coven's totem animals and symbols, Goddess and God names, what ritual tools are used and their associations, plus any passwords or signs, and proclaimed to the four quarters and the Gods as a priest or priestess and witch. These elements are educational and reflect the initiate's new status.

Achievement initiations can be done as both self- and group initiations. Examples of both follow:

Achievement Self-Initiation

You will need the following items:

A small altar table
Your usual ritual tools

A new braided cord, sash, or badge of accomplishment or rank including colors and symbols meaningful to you

A list of accomplishments since the last initiation or dedication, including areas of knowledge learned, skills mastered, exercises practiced, and rituals performed

A copy of this ritual

Find a quiet, private, secure location where you will not be disturbed during the ritual. Remember to turn off all your phones and lock your doors if you have roommates. Dress for the ritual in your usual manner or go skyclad if that is your usual manner. Set up the altar and place the listed items on it. Take a moment to ground and center.

Begin by casting a protective circle as described in chapter 2, including an invocation to the four elements. Once the circle is complete, invoke the Goddess and God to be present at your ritual by saying:

O Gracious Goddess, you who admonishes us to keep pure and ever strive toward our highest ideals, I ask that you be present tonight in my ritual to witness the presentation of my accomplishments to date, guide me in knowing how best to further grow and serve you, and bless me as I undertake the next leg of my spiritual journey.

O Fierce and Nurturing God, Horned Consort to the Earth, our Mother, I ask that you be present tonight in my ritual to give me the courage, strength, and guidance to continue on my winding journey to Self, oneness with the Old Gods and with Nature Herself. As every Fall you sacrifice yourself to the greater good to be reborn in the Spring, assist me in sacrificing my fears and hesitations as I end one stage of my path and begin a new one. Blessed Be.

Take the list of accomplishments from your altar and walk to the center of your circle. Say:

O Gracious Goddess, Horned Consort, and Watchers of the Four Elements, I present to you the activities and accomplishments that I have made in your names. May they be acceptable.

Now go through and verbally proclaim each item on your list. You might say something like:

I undertook the study of tarot reading and mastered the meanings of the cards and three card layouts.

I diligently kept a daily regimen of meditation in a properly cast circle.

I performed a ritual and meditation for each phase of the moon for the past six months.

In recognition of my body as Divine, I quit smoking and reduced my coffee intake from three cups to one cup per day.

After you have completed the list, place the list back on the altar and say:

I ask that you accept these accomplishments as proof of my dedication and progress, and grant me the [add level you are seeking—for example, First Degree of Wicca].

Close your eyes, quiet your mind, and wait. Listen to your intuition, which is one of the voices of the Gods. It will let you know through a vision, a sign, a thought, or even just a general feeling of whether or not you have been deemed worthy of the degree you seek. If the answer is "no," then thank the Gods, close the circle, and go back to studying. Do not just finish the degree anyway and figure that no one knows. The Gods and your own heart will know and you will find that any real progress will stop from that point on. You'll be just fooling yourself and people will figure out that you are a fraud pretty quickly.

If the answer is "yes," then proceed by presenting yourself and donning your new badge of rank. It can be a new robe or cord for your robe, a sash, badge, staff, tabard, or whatever.

Once you have put on your new badge, go around to each of the four quarters and say:

Lords and Lady of the [North, East, South, or West], I accept the honor that you have granted me and pledge to use my new skills and knowledge with wisdom and compassion in the service of you and the Goddess and God. I dedicate myself to continued study and growth in the Craft of the Wise and the love of the Old Gods of nature. So mote it be!

After you have completed the circuit, thank the Goddess and God by saying:

O Gracious Goddess, giver of the mystery of life and death, I thank you for being present in my ritual tonight. Thank you for witnessing my presentation and accepting me as worthy to be advanced to the next degree. May I remember that you are always present everywhere to guide and assist me in living in harmony and balance with the cycles and forces of nature. Hail and farewell.

O Fierce and Nurturing God, Lord within ourselves whose name is Mystery of Mysteries, I thank you for being present in my ritual tonight. Thank you for witnessing my presentation and accepting me as worthy to be advanced to the next degree. May I remember that you are always present everywhere to guide and assist me in living with strength, justice, and harmony with the cycles and forces of nature. Hail and farewell.

Close the circle in your usual manner and the ritual is complete.

Example of a Group Achievement Initiation

The coven opens the circle as usual while the Candidate waits in an adjoining room. The circle should have an altar, which includes a cup of water, a bowl of salt, a black candle, and burning incense, plus any other ritual tools used by the tradition. The ritual has seven main ritual participants: the High Priestess, High Priest, Magister, and four Elemental Guardians. The Guardians should stand in their respective directions.

High Priestess (HPS): Coven Brothers and Sisters, our Dedicant Sister _____ has made suitable progress in the Craft of the Wise as to enable her to pass an examination in the required knowledge. She is now eligible for advancement to the First Elemental Degree of Earth. Brother Magister, please oversee the preparation of the initiate and when she is ready, give the customary alarm.

Magister retires from the room, closing the door, and prepares the Candidate by blindfolding her and giving her a small cauldron filled with dirt. Magister guides the Candidate to the door and knocks. The High Priest opens the door.

Magister (M): We seek entry Between the Worlds to the Pathways of the Old Gods.

High Priest (HP): You may enter.

HP opens door and admits them, then returns to the side of the HPS.

HPS: Sister _____, you have been a dedicant for the required year and a day. Your spiritual mentor has taught you the ways of the Craft as are available to you at this time. You have taken written tests and performed the required ritual tasks, and your mentor has now recommended you for initiation to the next degree and admission into our coven and our tradition. Is this what you desire?

Candidate: Yes.

HP: Before you can be admitted you must demonstrate before those assembled that you are indeed qualified and prepared for this mighty step.

The Candidate is now asked a series of questions about information she was taught in her previous year's studies. They could include questions about the history of Wicca and/or the tradition she is being initiated into, basic precepts, or at a higher level, very specific information about a particular topic such as the Secret Names of Power, recitation of particular invocations, and the like. After successfully answers to the questions, the ritual proceeds.

HPS: Sister _____, you have answered well and proven yourself worthy. Brother Magister, please escort our sister to the center of the circle facing to the North.

M escorts Candidate to the center of the circle, faces her to the North and causes her to kneel.

HP: Please repeat after me: I, _____, in the presence of the Mighty Ones, do solemnly swear to keep secret any and all information that has been conveyed to me or will be conveyed to me by this coven in the past, present, or future. I further promise that I will not reveal the identities of the members of this coven or any members of this Craft tradition to any person, Wiccan or otherwise, unless I already know him or her to be a member of this tradition and only then after having tried him or her by questions such as I have answered this night. Furthermore, I will not discuss or convey the secrets of this degree to any person within or without this tradition unless he or she has already attained this degree. I further promise that I will ever strive in my studies of the Art Magickal that I may continue to grow and perhaps one day number myself among the Elders of the Craft of the Wise. Lastly, I most solemnly vow to heed the Law of Three and to uphold the Wiccan Rede in all my undertakings with all beings in this world or the other. This dread oath I swear by the Earth on which I kneel. As is my will, so mote it be.

HPS: Sister _____, it is my pleasure to proclaim you to the Four Winds and in the presence of the Mighty Ones a Witch and Priestess of the First Degree. Brother Magister, please escort our sister to the four quarters to be consecrated by guardians of the elements.

Upon completion of the oath, the blindfold is removed and the Initiate is helped to stand. M escorts the Initiate to the East.

Guardian of Air (GA): By the Power of Air, with the aid of Paralda and the sylphs, I consecrate you with the element of Air so that your mind may be opened to the Mysteries of the Old Ways.

GA censes Initiate and places a kiss on her forehead. M escorts the Initiate to the South.

Guardian of Fire (GF): By the Power of Fire, with the aid of Djin and the salamanders, I consecrate you with the element of Fire so that your heart may be opened to the Mysteries of the Old Ways.

GF waves a lit candle around the Initiate and places a kiss over her heart. M escorts the Initiate to the West.

Guardian of Water (GW): By the Power of Water, with the aid of Niksa and the undines, I consecrate you with the element of Water so that your Center may be opened to the Mysteries of the Old Ways.

GW sprinkles the Initiate with water and places a kiss over her womb. M escorts the Initiate to the North.

Guardian of Earth (GE): By the Power of Earth, with the aid of Ghob and the gnomes, I consecrate you with the element of Earth so that your body may be opened to the Mysteries of the Old Ways.

GE sprinkles the Initiate with salt and places a kiss in the palms of each hand. M escorts the Initiate back to the center of the circle.

HPS: Beloved Sister, for the duration of this ritual you have been holding in your hands a small cauldron filled with dirt. This cauldron is a symbol of the Earth, the Cauldron of Ceridwen, which is the Holy Grail of Immortality. This degree and the studies that will follow are all related to the element of Earth.

Here the HPS with the help of the other coveners present the Initiate with an overview of the coven's symbols, associations, and uses for the element of Earth. During the following year the student will be given the specific rituals, exercises, and in-depth information to master this degree. After the presentation, the circle is closed as usual. If there are parts of the opening and closing that are at a level above the Initiate's current degree, she will be escorted out before the closing.

The first example given was more eclectic in Wiccan style, whereas the second was much more ceremonial. However, notice that despite their stylistic differences, both had the essential elements of:

Demonstrating/proclaiming qualifications for advancement
The granting of a new status/degree
A commitment to continue training and study

These are the hallmarks of achievement focused initiations.

Transformative Initiations

Transformative initiations are rituals that are specifically designed to rattle your cage. To truly change and grow, we often have to be shaken out of our comfort zone. Our society places a high value on thought. Therefore, many of us pride ourselves on our rational capabilities and spend a great deal of time thinking about things. We think through our beliefs and create a rational worldview to justify and rationalize them. Every time we are introduced to a new concept, we set our minds to finding ways to fit the new idea into our existing worldview. However, transformation is not about modifying our existing world. It is about radically changing it or even throwing out the old altogether in favor of a radically different one. Thus, to get past our tendency to over think things and try to make them fit, transformative rituals are designed to evoke powerful emotions by accessing our other ways of processing information: physical sensation, emotion, imagination, impulse, and intuition.

The most common technique for getting around our thinking minds and the concepts that we've created about ourselves, the world, and our place in it—also called our "ego"—is through trials and challenges. Transformative rituals, which besides initiations also include "brainwashing" techniques, psychotherapeutic reprogramming, and military boot camp, all seek to first put the initiate into a state of vulnerability. In boot camp, the vulnerability takes the form of stripping a person's identity with the hair cutting, identical clothing, the yelling, and the random late night drills. The soldier is at the whim of the drill sergeant. Brainwashers often isolate people in a room and deprive them of food, sleep, exercise, and any other outside stimuli not controlled by the brainwasher. The most common way to do this in Wiccan and other initiatic groups is to blindfold and bind candidates, lead them through disorienting movements, and then to subject them to apparently life-threatening trials beyond their control.

The purpose of this is that when we become this vulnerable, our brains kick into a survival mode. We forget about our social status, our philosophical theories, our egos, and other noncritical functions. We simply want to survive. And like a newborn baby who is also vulnerable and at the whim of outsiders, we will bond to whatever entities give us nurturance, even if those entities are the same ones who made us vulnerable in the first place.

Once the bond is set, and while we are still open, and again just like parents do to children, the entities provide us with the specialized symbols, concepts, skills, worldview, and jargon of the group we are becoming members of. In the military, that is the language of weapons and military vehicles, codes of conduct, and other specialized military jargon. In Wicca, it is the tables of elemental associations, the specialized words like "athame" and "widdershins," the Gods and Goddesses, and the other theological and philosophical concepts. Thus, the most common approach in transformative initiations is to make initiates vulnerable and then while they are open, to present them with a series of images, symbols, and concepts from the new worldview being introduced. Until the initiate learns the language of this new worldview, and for the noninitiated, this array of symbols will seem random and irrational. And this is where the Mystery of mystery religions enters, for without the opening up and download of new symbol systems, the information does not make sense. It is only by being opened that these things make sense and great changes and insights can occur—the Mystery.

In most initiatic groups, after the initiation the student engages in extensive study of the information presented and thus implants the new information into the budding new worldview. Eventually, once the student has mastered the information of that level, additional initiations are administered to break down further preinitiatic concepts and introduce new ones in their stead.

Now this all may sound creepy and manipulative, but as I have tried to show, this is the way in which we all originally learn from our parents, school, the military, and society at large. If we are ever going to get real change, and not just additions or sidebars to our current beliefs about reality, then we need transformative rituals. For if we truly want to change our selves and our lives, we have to change our minds and basic assumptions about how the universe works.

As before, transformative rituals can be done either as a self-initiation or as a group initiation. It is a little harder doing transformative rituals for oneself since by their very nature they are supposed to make us vulnerable and then imprint new information and if we make up and perform the ritual on ourselves, how are we going to imprint things we don't already know if we don't know them to put in?

In this situation, the usual method in our culture is to put oneself at some limited or controlled danger and then open up for the intuition and insight that comes through while in that state. Good examples of this are modern vision quests, where a person goes out into a wild and dangerous place with minimal life supports and stays for several days waiting for a vision. However, it should be noted that most responsible vision questers do so with a guide along, who camps nearby in case of emergency. The team of quester and guide decide on a sign that all is okay, for example, the standing up of a rock that the quester performs every day at a set time, such as 10:00 A.M. The guide then makes a point of checking the sign every day after the set time, such as 11:00 A.M. If the sign is present, the guide resets the sign, in this case by laying the rock back down onto its side, so that the quester knows that it has been checked and the guide will know if it changes or not. If the sign is not present—the rock is still lying on its side at 11:00 A.M.—the quester takes this as a sign of trouble and mounts a rescue search.

In more traditional societies, these trials are often done without the safety net and thus are only done by the most serious of seekers. Success means deep transformation into a special class of spiritual leader, a shaman, or similar role. Failure often means death.

Example of a Wiccan Transformative Self-Initiation

This ritual is inspired by one of the traditional trials undertaken by aspiring bards in Celtic-speaking countries. Because we do not want to have any casualties, we are going to bring in safeguards and assistants to minimize the chance for serious injury.

You will need the following items and assistants:

One or more strong friends
A large blanket
Four ratcheting tie-down straps
Eight tent stakes large enough to fit the tie-down straps
Several heavy stones and/or cement blocks

The preparation for this ritual should last one full cycle of the moon. Beginning on the new moon, commence a six-week period of fasting and self-discipline. The self-discipline can be a regular period of meditation and study and the avoidance of something commonly done, enjoyed, or encountered. Examples include stopping drinking soda, watching television, or, more severely, using pronouns such as "he" and "she."

At the end of the six weeks, on the night of the full moon, just before dusk, go into an old cemetery. If you are in an urban area where doing such a thing might get you arrested, any isolated, outdoor place will do. Lie on a grave and have one of your assistants wrap a tie-down strap around your ankles, just above your knees, around your waist and wrists, chest and upper arms. The goal is to bind you tight enough that you can hardly move. Have your assistants stake the ends of the tie-down straps to the ground, pinning you in place. Next, have them cover you with the blanket, leaving the ends of it spread out on the ground. The cement blocks are then placed on top of the blanket around your body, again, pinning you and the blanket in place.

After you are in place, your assistants should leave so that you will be all alone. Depending on your comfort level, you may want to have them check on you once or twice in the night, or not at all. Less is better. But if they do, they should only stop by, ask you if you are all right, and then quickly leave again. There should be no hanging out, chatting, or interacting in any other way.

Alone in the cemetery, your job is to keep awake and to see what visions come to you. As a traditional bardic ritual, you would be required to recite epic poetry all evening. You don't want to just fall asleep or daydream while there. Instead, meditate on keeping your mind alert and open. If thoughts or emotions, such as boredom or fear, arise, you should observe them but do not allow yourself to quit early. Be present, awake, and open in whatever happens.

After dawn, your assistants should arrive to let you loose. Do not talk about your experiences with them. After you have packed up, go back to your home and record your experiences in your journal. Meditate and reflect on what happened for another cycle of the moon before discussing it with anyone.

Example of Transformative Group Initiation

As mentioned earlier, group-led transformative rituals have all the elements of transformative ritual, plus the benefit of the truly unknown. That is, it places the initiate into a state of heightened awareness, usually through creating a sense of vulnerability, and then implants into the initiate's unconscious a set of symbols, images, and ideas that will form the core of his or her new, transformed worldview.

Items you will need include:

Anointing oil
Athame (ritual knife)
Chalice
Wand
Sharp stone
Sword

The coven opens the circle as usual while the initiate waits in an adjoining room. The Candidate, who has fasted for the last twenty-four hours, is dressed in a simple white robe with a white cord around the waist. She is blindfolded and her feet and hands are bound. The altar is set up as usual. The High Priest has a sword for opening and closing the circle. The ritual has seven main ritual participants: the High Priestess, High Priest, Magister, and four Elemental Guardians. The Guardians should stand in their respective directions.

Magister (M) brings the Candidate into the room and leads her in walking backward counterclockwise around the circle. One full revolution of the circle is made before stopping at the Guardian of the West (GW), who presses the sharp edge of a chalice rim to the candidate's chest.

GW: Who comes here?

M (for Candidate): One who is lost in the Darkness. A seeker groping in the darkness searching for the path of the Mighty Ones, the God and Goddess, and the love and light that they bring.

GW: What are you willing to sacrifice to pass the gate of the West?

M (for Candidate): My fear.

GW: I will take your fear and other limiting emotions. Pass on with neither hope nor fear in your heart.

GW anoints the Candidate with an oil on each shoulder and at the top of the pelvic bone. M brings her to the South, still walking backward, stopping at the Guardian of the South (GS), who presses the point of an athame into the Candidate's chest.

GS: Who comes here?

M (for Candidate): One who is lost in the Darkness. A seeker groping in the darkness searching for the path of the Mighty Ones, the God and Goddess, and the love and light that they bring.

GS: What are you willing to sacrifice to pass the gate of the South?

M (for Candidate): My desire.

GS: I will take your desire and ambition. Unbridled desire becomes impulsiveness and blindness. Pass on without expectation.

GS anoints the Candidate with an oil on each breast and the forehead. M brings her to the East, stopping at the Guardian of the East (GE), who presses the point of a wand into the Candidate's chest.

GE: Who comes here?

M (for Candidate): One who is lost in the Darkness. A seeker groping in the darkness searching for the path of the Mighty

Ones, the God and Goddess, and the love and light that they bring.

GE: What are you willing to sacrifice to pass the gate of the East?

M (for Candidate): My previous knowledge.

GE: I will take your thoughts, beliefs, and your name. Only by abandoning what we "think" we know can we be open to receiving new knowledge without judgment. Pass on with an open mind.

GE anoints both palms of the Candidate's hands. M brings her to the North, stopping at the Guardian of the North (GN), who presses the edge of a sharp stone into the Candidate's chest.

GN: Who comes here?

M (for Candidate): One who is lost in the darkness. A seeker groping in the darkness searching for the path of the Mighty Ones, the God and Goddess, and the love and light that they bring.

GN: What are you willing to sacrifice to pass the gate of the North?

M (for Candidate): My whole body.

GN: I will take the sum of your body. Only by fully devoting your every cell, action, thought, feeling, and breath to the God and Goddess can you ever hope to walk the paths of the Craft of the Wise. Pass on.

GN anoints both of the Candidate's feet. M brings her to the edge of the circle. HP uses a sword to open the circle and admit M and the Candidate. HP closes the circle and M escorts the Candidate to the center of the circle and helps her to lie on the floor.

HPS: Welcome, Child of Darkness. You have given away your emotions. You have given away your desires. You have given away your thoughts and previous beliefs. You have even given away your name in the world. Lastly, you have given away the very cells of your body. You are nothingness, floating once again in the dark comforting womb of the Goddess. Imagine yourself floating there, gently rocking in the warm, nurturing amniotic fluid of the Divine. Imagine a gentle pressing on your sides, a squeezing and a rushing down a narrow tunnel toward a bright light. Emerge into the bright light and feel yourself nestled into the warm breast of the Mother of All. See her gazing down at you. Look at her face. Take in all its details. In your mind, ask her what your name is and listen for her reply. Ask her what your new life's purpose is—what is your task in the Craft of the Wise. Listen for her answer. Thank her and feel her love for you and all of the world. Close your eyes again and feel the warmth of her embrace. Gather up that warmth and store it in your heart region. Open your eyes, Child of Light and welcome to the Craft of the Wise.

The Initiate is now led around the circle and introduced to the symbols of the four directions, the ritual tools, and any other appropriate information. The circle is then closed in the usual manner.

Combined Achievement/ Transformative Initiations

Frequently, initiations will include both achievement and transformative portions. In many traditions, they are done sequentially, that is, first the initiate's achievement in mastering the previous training is recognized, followed by a transformative initiation that opens the initiate to the new symbolic information to be imparted.

These combined initiations are most commonly done as group rituals; however, it is not impossible to do a combined self-initiation. The typical format would be to do an achievement ceremony like that presented earlier, followed by a vision quest.

Combined group initiations would follow a similar format. The first section would be a recognition of previous accomplishment and qualification to proceed with the second section. The second section would then be a challenging transformative initiation where the initiate is made vulnerable, undergoes a symbolic death and resurrection, and is then presented with the new symbols and knowledge of the next degree.

Example of Combined Group Initiation

Items needed:

Small bowl of water for sprinkling the candidate
Medium-sized basin of water
Large ladle
Large basin of water
Towel
Blindfold
2 black cords each 3 feet long
Large blanket
Dull knife
Various symbols of Water
Usual altar and circle ritual tools

The coven opens the circle as usual while the initiate waits in an adjoining room. The ritual has seven main ritual participants: the High Priestess, High Priest, Maiden, and four Elemental Guardians. The Guardians should stand in their respective directions.

High Priest (HP): Coven Brothers and Sisters, our Brother _____ has made suitable progress in the Elemental Degree of Earth as to enable him to pass an examination in the required knowledge. He is now eligible for advancement to the Second Elemental Degree of Water. Sister Maiden, please oversee the preparation of the initiate and when he is ready, give the customary alarm.

Maiden retires from the room, closing the door, and prepares the Candidate by blindfolding him and giving him a small vial filled with water. Maiden guides the Candidate to the door and knocks. The High Priestess opens the door.

Maiden (M): We seek passage to the Realm of Water.

High Priestess (HPS): You may enter.

HPS opens door and admits them, then returns to the side of the HP.

HP: Brother _____, you have labored in the Realm of Earth for the required year and a day. Your spiritual mentor has taught you the secret knowledge and rite of Earth as practiced in our tradition. You have taken written tests and performed the required ritual tasks, and your mentor has now recommended you for initiation to the next degree. Is this what you desire?

Candidate: Yes.

HPS: Before you can be admitted you must demonstrate before those assembled that you are indeed qualified and prepared for this mighty step.

The Candidate is now asked a series of questions about information he was taught in his previous year's studies. In this instance, they could include questions about which astrological signs are Earth signs, the magickal properties of various stones, incenses and herbs of Earth, how one performs geomantic divination, the names of various Earth symbols, and other Tradition-specific associations and information. After successful answers to the questions, the ritual proceeds.

HP: Brother _____, you have answered well and proven yourself worthy. Sister Maiden, please escort our brother to the center of the circle facing to the North.

M escorts the Candidate to the center of the circle, faces him to the North, and causes him to kneel.

HPS: Please repeat after me: I, _____, in the presence of the Mighty Ones, do solemnly swear as I have previously done, to keep secret any and all information that has been conveyed to me or will be conveyed to me by this coven in the past, present, or future. I further promise that I will not reveal the identities of the members of this coven or any members of this Craft tradition to any person, Wiccan or otherwise, unless I already know him or her to be a member of this tradition and only then after having tried him or her by questions such as I have answered this night. Furthermore, I will not discuss or convey the secrets of this degree to any person within or without this tradition unless he or she has already attained this degree. I further promise that I will ever strive in my studies of the Art Magickal that I may continue to grow and perhaps one day number myself among the Elders of the Craft of the Wise. Lastly, I most solemnly vow to heed the Law of Three and to uphold the Wiccan Rede in all my undertakings with all beings in this world or the other. This dread oath I swear by the blood coursing through my veins and the tears that will shed should I violate these oaths. As is my will, so mote it be.

HP: Brother _____, it is my pleasure to proclaim you to the Four Winds and in the presence of the Mighty Ones a Witch and Priest of the Second Degree. Sister Maiden, please escort our brother to the four quarters to be consecrated by guardians of the elements.

Upon completion of the oath, the blindfold is removed and the Initiate is helped to stand. M escorts the Initiate to the East.

Eastern Guardian of Air (EG): By the Power of Air, with the aid of Raphael, Lord of Air, I consecrate you with the element of Air so that your mind may be opened to the Mysteries of the Old Ways.

EG censes the Initiate and places a kiss on his forehead. M escorts the Initiate to the South.

Southern Guardian of Fire (SG): By the Power of Fire, with the aid of Michael, Lord of Fire, I consecrate you with the element of Fire so that your heart may be opened to the Mysteries of the Old Ways.

SG waves a lit candle around the Initiate and places a kiss over his heart. M escorts the Initiate to the West.

Western Guardian of Water (WG): By the Power of Water, with the aid of Gabriel, Lord of Water, I consecrate you with the element of Water so that your center may be opened to the Mysteries of the Old Ways.

WG sprinkles the Initiate with water and places a kiss about two inches below his navel. M escorts the Initiate to the North.

Northern Guardian of Earth (NG): By the Power of Earth, with the aid of Uriel, Lord of Earth, I consecrate you with the element of Earth so that your body may be opened to the Mysteries of the Old Ways.

GE sprinkles the Initiate with salt and places a kiss in the palms of each hand. M escorts the Initiate back to the center of the circle.

HP: Beloved Brother, for the duration of this ritual you have been holding in your hands a small vial filled with water. This small sample of water is symbolic of the great element of Water, the amniotic Void from whence we came and to which we return when we cross the Veil into the Otherworld.

HPS: You will now be escorted back to the anteroom for further preparation. Upon your return, you will travel the dangerous byways of the Watery Realm.

The Initiate is escorted back into the anteroom, where he is stripped naked, his hands and feet bound by a black cord, and blindfolded again by the Maiden. While this is taking place, the ritual team is rearranging the ritual room for this second section. When the ritual preparations are done, the HP opens the door and brings the Initiate back into the room and circle, closing the boundary of the circle after entering.

HPS: In the time before time, there existed the Void, the great endless depths of dark Water, and all was Chaos, the mindless swirlings and eddies of Nothingness.

The Initiate is escorted to the East, where EG dips fingers into a small bowl and sprinkles him with water.

EG: Rain, the teardrops of the Gods, that purify and enliven.

M escorts the Initiate to the South. He is made to bend over with his head over a large basin of water. SG ladles three large ladles full of water over the Initiate's head.

SG: Bubbling streams of passion and desire that propel into action and change.

M escorts the Initiate to the West. His whole head is dunked briefly into a large basin of water by WG. Some words of assurance such as "This is going to be very wet, but just relax and everything will be okay" may be needed before just dunking the person's head so that he knows that something is coming. M places a towel over the Initiate's head and shoulders.

WG: The deep oceans of feeling, the vast depths of our subconscious hopes, fears, and desires.

M escorts the Initiate to the North. NG takes a dull blade and runs it over both of the Initiate's wrists hard enough so that he feels it, but no blood is drawn.

NG: Blood, the pulsing waters of life that flow through our veins.

HP: Escort the candidate to the rest of darkness to return to the Watery Void of Death.

M escorts the Initiate to the center of the circle, where he lays down on a blanket on the floor, which is then wrapped around him tightly, leaving just room enough for him to breathe. The Initiate is left to just lie in the darkness and silence for several minutes.

HPS: And the King of Gods, Marduk, armed with his net, bow, and arrow strove in single combat with Great Tiamat, Mother of All. He slew her and split her like a shellfish into two parts: half of her he made into the earth below and half he set up as the sky, holding back the Waters of Chaos and the Void. Thus, the World was born.

M removes the blindfold and HP assists in unwrapping the Initiate and helping him to rise to a sitting position.

HPS: Like a babe born from the waters of the primordial womb, arise!

M and HP assist the Initiate to rise to his feet. HP with the help of the other coveners present the Initiate with various signs, symbols, and images and other items associated with the element of Water. During the following year the student will be given the specific rituals, exercises, and in-depth information to master this degree. After the presentation, the circle is closed as usual. If there are parts of the opening and closing that are at a level above the Initiate's current degree, he will be escorted out before the closing.

A Multitude of Degrees

There is a large variance in the number of degrees and initiations that different groups use. Some groups don't have initiations at all. Other groups have anywhere from one to ninety-nine degrees. The reason for these variations is usually based on the primary symbol system and organizational structure used by the group.

Nonhierarchical groups usually do not have a progressive system of degrees. Therefore, they usually do not have formal initiations of any kind. Instead, because their rituals are usually less structured and more spontaneous, initiatic rituals tend to be undertaken only as the need naturally arises in a person. That is, if in the course of a person's life he or she finds him- or herself undergoing a natural rite of passage—for example, the leaving home of the last child—then an achievement-type rite of passage might be performed by the group to help the person mark this change and move onto the next step of his or her life. Similarly, if the person seems stuck in some way, then the group may help him or her to undergo some sort of challenge and transformative ritual to get him or her out of his or her rut and initiate a new way of living. This same system could work very well for solitary practitioners as well.

Groups that do have formal initiations usually use them for different reasons. Groups with only one initiation essentially are using the ritual as a dedication to the group. Typically, their organizational structure is similar to nonhierarchical groups and thus the initiation is simply the rite of passage of joining the group. Any other initiations would be as needed or wanted.

A few groups do only two main initiations. Typically, the first initiation marks the candidate's entry into an "outer order" of the group, where he or she receives the majority of his or her training. This is similar to the dedication ritual described earlier. Once the student has proven him- or herself capable of learning and being harmonious with the group, then a second initiation is performed to welcome him or her into full membership in the "inner order" of the group.

Most groups that use a three-degree system or a multiple thereof (9, 27, 33, 66, 99) are either Masonic or come from a Masonic-influenced tradition. British Traditional Wicca and all the groups spun off or influenced by it, various schools of Druidry, and a host of esoteric orders are all Masonic influenced and thus use variations of a three-degree system.

Groups that use a four-degree system are typically based on the four elements of Earth, Air, Fire, and Water. The degrees in such systems are explorations of each of these elements individually. Occasionally, such groups will have a fifth degree that represents the union of the four elements or Spirit.

Groups with a ten-degree system are often based on the qabalah, especially as configured by the Hermetic Order of the Golden Dawn. In these groups, each degree marks one of the sephiroth on the Tree of Life.

Interestingly, the Hermetic Order of the Golden Dawn uses a combined two-, four-, and ten-degree system. The candidate takes the first degree, which is the entry into the outer order. Next follows four elemental degrees corresponding with the sephiroth of Malkuth, Yesod, Hod, and Netzach on the Tree of Life. Upon successful completion of the four elemental degrees and approval from members of the inner order, the student undergoes a unifying portal degree giving entrance into the inner order. The next three degrees, symbolizing the next three sephiroth of Tiphareth, Geburah, and Chesed, each contain four subdegrees corresponding with the four elements again. The final three degrees, representing the top supernal sephiroth on the Tree of Life, Binah, Chokmah, and Kether, are not attainable by incarnate beings. There is also a system of threes in this degree system (three sets of three sephiroth corresponding with various Masonic principles, plus the bottom sephiroth of Malkuth, which is the material world), just to make the whole more complicated.

In my experience, initiatic groups with more than ten degrees are often engaged in ritual theater, which is a learning tool different than an initiation, or achievement initiations. Realistically, since each transformative initiation is designed to be earth-shaking for the initiate, it would take a superhuman amount of fortitude, and not just a little masochism, to undergo twenty to one hundred such initiations.

There are certainly other variations on the number and type of subsequent degrees based on principles not mentioned here. The important point is that since most initiatic systems have the goal of transforming the candidate and his or her worldview, the number and type of degrees usually reflects that new worldview. As an adept actively engaged in personal transformation for yourself and others, you want to make sure that there is consistency between your symbol system, organizational structure, group intention, and initiatic system. This will help you to ensure that the ritual has the intended effect with maximum capacity for creating change. This is particularly important since the next stage of your work involves transforming yourself in a very specific way to make yourself suitable for Divine possession.

CHAPTER 7

A Sacred Vessel: Deity Work and Divine Possession

*T*he coven is gathered in its sacred circle. Heavy incense wafts through
the air as the candles flicker in time with the swaying of bodies and
the rhythm of the chanting. In the middle of the circle sits a small middle-
aged woman in flowing robes. Her eyes are shut and she is also swaying
with the chanting. The chant reaches a crescendo and at its very peak the
robed priestess yells, "Come Great Hecate into your servant!" Everyone
falls silent and still. As the coven members watch the priestess, an appre-
ciative gasp escapes their lips. For although the person sitting in the middle
still looks the same, she also looks different. Somehow she seems to be both
small and yet over seven feet tall. Her graying hair now seems black, the
kind of black that seems to suck the light out of the room, not dissimilar
from the dark, new moon itself. Her eyes have a depth, a power, a wisdom,
and a gleam that was not there before. It is as if the coven members are
gazing into the eyes of an Ancient Being from before the dawn of time.
When she speaks, it is not in her usual quiet, tentative tones, but with the
force and power of one accustomed to being revered and worshipped. Her
words are few, but each is direct, clear, and touches to the core. The Goddess
is here.

"Drawing Down the Moon," also known as "aspecting" or "divine possession," is mentioned in several introductory books. As
an adept, one of your goals is to have a strong connection to the

Divine. There is no more powerful way of connecting with the Divine than through possession. However, since most covens reserve this powerful work for higher-level practitioners, very little is in print as to the specific types, levels, or techniques of divine possession in a Wiccan context. This is very advanced work and should be gone into slowly and carefully. In that vein, let's start by being clear about the terms and concepts involved.

Definitions

When reading or talking about deity work with Wiccan teachers, the student is often barraged with a variety of terms and concepts. So let's start off our exploration by looking at what is meant by these terms.

"Divine possession" is a state in which a person is inhabited and under varying levels of control by a God, Goddess, or other spiritual being. This process, in turn, will displace all or part of the person's consciousness. In Wicca, this state is also sometimes called "carrying" and "deity assumption" to distinguish it from journeying, prayer, and other less intense methods of working with Gods or spirits.

"Aspecting" involves the priest or priestess taking on one "aspect" of a God, Goddess, or other spiritual being. For example, Inanna is both a love and warrior Goddess. A priest or priestess can take on only the love Goddess version of Inanna if it best suits a ritual's intent. Aspecting can range from a person simply representing the God or Goddess symbolically by dressing up and playing the role to the various levels of actual possession. As we will see later, this approach is more common in pantheistic Wiccans than polytheistic ones.

"Drawing Down the Moon" or "Drawing Up the Sun" are the common names for the process a Wiccan takes to aspect or carry deity. Drawing Down usually refers to bringing a Goddess into a person and Drawing Up usually refers to bringing in a God. Once a person is possessed, he or she is commonly referred to as "drawn down."

"Invocation" means to call in something. In this case, it refers to the calling of deity or spirit to enter and inhabit a space, object, or person.

"Evocation" literally means to "call up, elicit, or draw forth." This refers to drawing spirits out of an object, place, or person so that they can be interacted with.

"Trance" is an altered state of consciousness distinct from our ordinary, wakeful awareness. Other altered states include sleep, coma, and drug-induced states, none of which is trance. Many people think of trance as a highly focused, quieting, inner focus of attention and awareness, but trance can also be very expansive, energizing, and active. Each trance state has its uses and is induced through different techniques that will be discussed later.

The relationship between these terms is sometimes complex. Trance is often used as a means of preparing for deity work, and being possessed could be called an altered or trance state. However, not all trances lead to deity assumption. Trance can be used by itself to stimulate states of higher consciousness and awareness of the surrounding energies. Nor is it necessary for deity assumption. It is also not entirely uncommon for someone to be divinely possessed without being in a prior trance state of any kind. However, trance can greatly enhance the likelihood of successful deity work, especially for those inexperienced in it.

One invocation technique that usually uses trance as a prerequisite is Drawing Down the Moon. Few Wiccans actually use evocation in deity work. That is, they seldom call the Divine out of some object, even though they could. Unless the person has been spontaneously possessed, representing a deity in ritual is usually just acting unless some level of trance state is present. Once a trance state exists, the person is probably aspecting. Depending on the depth of the aspecting, and in part the theological beliefs of the person, divine possession or carrying can happen. However, not all aspecting is carrying since aspecting can be symbolic only.

Theological Models

If we're going to be working with deities or the Divine, it is important to know that not everyone sees things the same way, even among Wiccans. I'll present some of the major models in use, but please bear in mind that many witches use a combination of approaches. There is a saying: get three Wiccans together and you'll have at least five different opinions.

"Monotheism" is the belief in, and worship of, only one all-encompassing God. Usually, the God is a creator who made the world and thus there is a Divine spark in all things. However, the God does not live there. While most people are aware that this is the Judeo-Christian model, they aren't always aware that other religions often have sects that are monotheist, including Wicca. The Frost's Church of Wicca is one such example. There are witches who worship only one Divine being but choose to see it as either a Goddess or simply a sexless Being. Some monotheistic Pagans, in particular Quaker Pagans, choose not to personify the One at all.

"Pantheism" is the belief that identifies the Divine as present in all matter. All matter is the sum of the Divine fully manifest. In this regard, all Gods are one God, all Goddesses are one Goddess, and the God and Goddess are One. Similarly, we are all part of that immanent deity. This differs some from the monotheist belief because the Divine, while still being ultimately One, is not so much the distinct creator of our world as the sum of all its seen and unseen parts. Each person or thing is fully a part or aspect of the One like the pieces of a puzzle. For this reason, it is fully acceptable to work with just one "aspect" of that One Divine, be it a particular cultural Goddess such as Inanna, or a more general aspect of divine feminine referred to as "the Goddess."

"Panentheism" is the belief that the Divine is present in all matter but that there still exists a part of the Divine that is apart and separate from all matter. All matter is part of the Divine, but is not the sum of the Divine. This is a mix of monotheism and pantheism. Like pantheism, it says that all of creation is fully imbued with and part of the Divine One, but that the One is still a creator who exists outside of and is independent of creation.

"Polytheism" is the belief in, or worship of, more than one God or Goddess as a distinct entity. Unlike any of the previously discussed beliefs, polytheists literally believe in distinct, unrelated Gods and Goddesses. Like people, they each have their own unique personalities, likes, dislikes, and ways of being approached. They cannot be mixed, matched, or combined. Many polytheists work with a set of Gods and Goddesses specific to a particular time period and culture. Examples would include pre-Christian Norse pantheons, ancient Attic Greek pantheons, and ancient Sumerian pantheons.

"Henotheism" is the worship of one particular God or Goddess without disbelieving or denying the existence of other Gods or Goddesses. Some polytheists choose to serve only one God or Goddess, such as Aphrodite, but in doing so do not deny the existence of others.

"Animism" is the concept that all elements of Nature have a spiritual consciousness. That is, all things including rocks and atoms have spirits that can be communicated and worked with. Similarly, all things need to be shown the same respect as you would any other conscious being.

"Nontheism" is the belief in a sacred, divine universe devoid of Gods or spirits. For example Taoism believes in a sacred set of principles and patterns that simply exist and have always existed. The goal of human spiritual practices should be to attune oneself to those patterns and principles, thus creating harmony and balance in one's life and with the world. Occasionally, some nontheist groups will believe in Gods and spirits, but simply see them as other beings not so different from people, plants, and animals that are trying to find balance. They are to be respected like neighbors, but not to be worshipped.

"Atheism" is the belief that there is no God, Divine, or spirits of any sort. Everything is a matter of chemistry, physics, and chance.

How Your Model Impacts the Way You Work with the Divine

Different theological models have different effects on how one works with the Divine. Atheists, of course, wouldn't work with the Divine at all. Nontheists wouldn't work with Gods and Goddesses, but with trying to become One with the patterns and plans of the universe. Therefore, they wouldn't do invocations to Gods, but would try to bring themselves more and more into awareness and harmony of the cosmic forces. Monotheists would work with only one God or Goddess and because the Divine is outside of us, they would tend to do work to bring the Divine into themselves. Panentheists, believing all is the Divine but that the Divine extends beyond creation, could both invoke the Divine into themselves but also might seek the Divine within themselves and try to bring it out into awareness. Pantheists would feel free to invoke a variety of Gods and Goddesses, often at the same time. Polytheists recoil at invocations to "the Goddess" because they do not believe in a single unified One, and thus an invocation to "the Goddess" is an open invitation to any Goddess, some of which might not be friendly. At the very least, such an invocation would be like always referring to your partner as "woman" rather than her name, which she might take offense at over time. Similarly, just as not all people, especially ones from widely different cultures, get along on friendly terms, so one would have to be very careful invoking Gods and Goddesses from various pantheons. Two warrior Gods from different cultures might either become drinking buddies during the ritual or wage open war. Neither may fit your ritual plans.

Sources of the Divine:
Invocation vs. Evocation

Once you have figured out what your theological model is, the next step is to figure out where you expect to find the Divine. As mentioned earlier, invocation is the calling into one's self a God, Goddess, or spirit, whereas evocation is the calling out of one's self, or some item, place, or thing, a God, Goddess, or spirit. If you are a monotheist where the Divine is outside of creation, you would probably do an invocation to bring it into yourself. If you are pantheist or panentheist where the Divine is within all things, you could do either an invocation or evocation. You could invoke the Divine spark from outside in the form of Nature, the land, the Goddess, or just the pool of collective Divine. Or you could connect with the Divine spark in yourself and evoke it into consciousness. Because polytheists or henotheists would see their Gods as distinct entities from each other and from humans, they would almost certainly rely primarily on invocations to bring those Gods into themselves. Animists would often use evocations to interact with the spiritual consciousness of the things around them. Nontheists and atheists would most likely avoid invocations and evocations all together as anything other than poetry. There are, of course, multiple combinations of these approaches such as an animistic polytheist. As long as they are compatible, the general principles laid out earlier still apply.

Levels of Possession

There are many ways to conceptualize the various levels of trance and possession. In reality, it is a spectrum that runs from nontranced through varying depths to very deep trance. At each level of trance, there are levels of deity work and possession possible. One useful way to conceptualize these levels has been presented by Judy Harrow and Mevlannen Beshderen. The following is essentially their model, and is modified where I have a different experience.

According to Harrow and Beshderen, there are four levels of trance, each with a concurrent level of deity and possession work.

Enhancement Trance

This trance level is the most shallow. Here, the priest or priestess feels the presence of the Divine. He or she feels enhanced, a little more powerful than usual. It is often experienced as a mantle of power being laid on his or her shoulders. I have also heard it described as if the God or Goddess were standing behind you with his or her hands on your shoulders. Someone who is trying to aspect a deity, that is, trying to represent a God or Goddess in a ritual, may feel him- or herself empowered and as if he or she has taken on an aura of authority. If your body was a car and your mind was your consciousness, you would be alone driving the car, but you would be confident because you knew that you had gotten great directions from the Gods.

Inspiration Trance

At this deeper level of trance, the priest or priestess now feels the actual presence of the God or Goddess nearby. But now, instead of just lending his or her presence to the priest or priestess, he or she is speaking directly to the priest or priestess and giving guidance. This guidance can literally be a whisper in the ear, a vision, impulse, intuition, sensation, or just a "knowing" of what to do or say. To use the car analogy, you are still alone driving the car, but now you have the God or Goddess on the cell phone giving you direct, real-time direction.

Integration Trance

This level is where actually "carrying" begins. At this level, the God or Goddess has actually entered the priest's or priestess's body. To use the car image, he or she is now riding in the passenger seat of the car with one hand on the wheel. At times, the Divine might even take the wheel and put you in the passenger seat. This state is often one of split-vision. You are in your body speaking, talking, acting, but someone else is also in there occasionally speaking, talking, and acting too. People with lots of experience with Divine possession find that this state becomes a fairly easy one to slip in and out of. It is not uncommon to be speaking to a Wiccan elder and suddenly see someone else speaking to you—someone big, powerful, ancient, and wise. He or she usually tells you something very profound and poignant and then as quickly as it came, the God or Goddess is gone and you are back talking to the elder again. It can be unnerving the first couple of times you are on either the giving or receiving end.

Possession Trance

This is the deepest or highest level of trance. At this stage, you are no longer in control. You are in the backseat of the car. You can see it happening, but are powerless to do anything. At the deepest level, you are in the trunk of the car and will have no memory at all of what your body did or said. This is full possession, where your consciousness is fully displaced by the consciousness of the Divine. This state is only for highly trained Wiccans who have a strongly established and trusting relationship with one particular aspect of the Divine.

Typically, because each level of trance requires a greater giving up of personal control, the ritual structure and invocation/evocation techniques become more structured. This is for a couple closely related reasons. First, as you give up more control, it is important that the specific deity, terms of interaction, and such are increasingly more controlled. This way you know who will possess you, where and when it will happen, and what can and cannot happen. This provides a greater sense of safety, which leads directly into the second reason, which is that it is easier to let go of control over your own body and mind when you know that there are safeguards in the form of ritual technique and structure built into the process. Thus, there are several necessary stages of preparation and training required to engage in deity work and possession, each varying fairly widely depending on one's theological model, whether this is evocation or invocation, how deep one wants to go, and what level of experience one has.

Ethics of Divine Possession

One of the pieces of baggage that many people carry over to Wicca from their Christian upbringing is the assumption of the beneficence and omnificence of the Gods. Many people just assume that because something is "Otherworldly" or Divine that it is also benign and would never do anything to hurt you or those around you. Monotheists, pantheists, and panentheists are more likely to assume this than polytheists, but nonetheless I have seen all sorts of Pagans make this unconscious assumption. However, to do so has its own risks and perils. Thus, whenever working with Otherworldly beings, please remember the following two points:

First, Gods and other spirit beings are powerful. Just interacting with them runs risks regardless of your or their intentions. Interacting with them needs to be done with care and control. They may not intend to cause you harm, but they are just so naturally powerful that if you accidentally make strong contact with them when you aren't fully prepared in the proper way, you can get hurt.

In that regard, they are like electricity. Used carefully in a controlled manner, such as with insulated wires and electric outlets in your house, its energy can be harnessed and used for healthy, productive uses. However, without those safeguards, electricity can and will fry you, burn down your house, and possibly injure those around you, regardless of your or its intentions.

It is not uncommon for people who are just dabbling in working with Gods and Goddesses to suddenly find that their world has turned upside down. I have known priestesses working with love Goddesses to find their families broken up and themselves in entirely new relationships within a matter of weeks. While this might be better in the long run, it also brought the suffering of bitter separations, child custody battles, and more. I also know covens and groups that have worked with various "lame Gods," including Hephaestus, the crippled blacksmith God of Greek mythology, and Legba, the lame crossroads loa of Vodoun. In those cases, it was not uncommon for members to find themselves being marked by the Gods by becoming physically impaired themselves. Thus, it is always important to be careful about what kind of energy you are invoking around you, especially if you are not yet skilled in working with Divine energy.

Second, Gods and other spirit beings are not human. This may sound obvious, but the point is that we often assume, because we commonly envision them in human or human-like form, that they have ethics and boundaries similar to ours. Let me assure you that that is not the case. All you have to do is actually read the mythologies to get a sense of how their ethics differ from modern ethical standards.

Many ancient Gods required blood sacrifice. At the very least, many such as Thor, Aries, and Cuchulainn didn't see a problem with killing their enemies. Artemis's hunting pack had no problem tearing apart innocent humans who wandered into her path. Neither did Bachus's entranced maenads. Some Goddesses, such as Aphrodite, encouraged sacred prostitution. Zeus was a womanizer and pedophile.

Pretty much every God, and many of their practitioners in antiquity, has crossed the boundaries of modern society. And while this can be a good thing in that it encourages us to question and explore societal norms in regards to sexuality and social structures, when it comes to Divine possession, it needs to be gone into very carefully. I have known inexperienced priests who while possessed by a warrior God would hit people who irritated them. I have known priestesses of Aphrodite who have found themselves in sexual situations that they never would have gotten into otherwise and that had unwanted repercussions on their marriages. There was even a priest who had invoked Zeus and then had to be distracted and reigned in when he wanted to seduce the underage girl in the group. In Zeus's time, it was acceptable for him to have sex with minors, but not today. Afterward, the priest was horrified by his behavior and the group had a lot of emotional processing to do.

On a different note, Gods being essentially immortal, they might not see a problem with putting you into unsafe situations. And to them, if you die, so what? Everything dies. So it is critical to remember that Gods and other spirit beings have different ideas of what is and is not acceptable behavior than we do, and may or may not care about your safety.

Therefore, it is critical before working with Gods and possession that you do the following:

Know and clearly define your own boundaries around acceptable behavior. Before working with Divine possession, think long and deeply about how far is too far when it comes to behaviors during possession. If possessed, is it acceptable to find yourself sleeping with someone you may or may not know? Is it acceptable to find yourself sleeping with several others? The Gods and Goddesses are often lusty beings so be aware. What about finding yourself eating, drinking, or smoking things you normally wouldn't? How much change in your life is acceptable? What if you lose your job, your partner, your friends, your home, your health, perhaps even your sexual identity? How much are you willing to put into the hands of the Gods?

Know the Gods you will be working with. Before working with a specific God or Goddess, do an exhaustive study of that being. Read all the myths about him or her and read about him or her from different translations or more scholarly sources. Many popular books and high school texts on the myths take out most of the sex—especially the cross-dressing and homosexuality—and the violence. Research the artwork that has been done for that deity. Artists are often intuiting useful insight into the Gods that they paint. What feelings do you get when you look at their images.

When working with evocable beings, the research is a bit different. Typically, there are three types of beings that you would evoke:

- Nature spirits such as the spirit of a tree, rock, spring, or similar natural feature
- Some archetypal aspect of the Divine from within yourself, such as "the Hunter" or "the Healer"
- Your own inner Divine spark

In all these cases, there are no specific names, images, or myths associated with them. For research, the best you can do is to look into how others have characterized those aspects. If it is an archetype, you might want to research that archetype cross-culturally. How is the Divine healer represented around the world? How many different ways are there to hunt? For tree spirits, you might research the qualities, needs, and uses of the tree in question. Does it appear in literature? Does it have folklore references? Does it have any healing or nutritional qualities? For your inner Divine spark, how do others characterize the soul?

Designate a guardian or anchor. This is a person who will watch out for you during the possession. He or she should be fully aware of all your boundaries and be willing and able to ensure that you hold to them while possessed. Ideally, he or she will be able to foresee any possible situations that might be problematic and avoid them. For example, the naked dancing around a priest invoked with Pan is probably a bad idea if the priest has a boundary around sex with people in the group. At the least, he or she should be able to distract and redirect any errant impulses from the Gods. In extreme cases, he or she needs to be able to forcibly rip you out of your trance and possession. Having a guardian is your safety net.

He or she should also be the one to at least assist, if not perform, the opening and closing of your ritual. The guardian should open it because you want to be able to focus on your task ahead without worrying about the details. He or she should also close the ritual because if all goes according to plan, there is a good chance that you will be too tired or not fully reintegrated enough to close it. By having a guardian present, you can feel free to let go of worrying about logistics and safety, making it easier to allow the Divine to possess you.

To recap, the process of preparing for Divine possession includes several steps, some of which we've already touched on. Before moving onward, let's list the steps discussed so far:

1. Depending on your theological model, decide whether you want to evoke or invoke.
2. Pick a God or Goddess that you want to work with.
3. Perform exhaustive research on that God or Goddess.
4. Clearly define your own ethics and boundaries.
5. Select a guardian to be with you during your possession.

Setting Boundaries

Knowing your own boundaries and having a guardian to make sure that you don't cross them are important pieces to have in place before undertaking a Divine possession. It is also important that you have made those boundaries clear to the God or Goddess you plan on working with and feel comfortable that he or she knows and will abide by those boundaries. To do that, you need to have a "getting to know you" period with the God or Goddess.

Evocable Deities and Beings

Nature Spirits

After having done your research, bring yourself into the physical presence of the item, thing, or place from which you want to evoke. Sit next to the pool or tree, hold the stone, and touch the rock ledge containing the spirit you would like to evoke. Close your eyes and take a few moments to breathe, feeling your breath coming and going from your nostrils, causing your chest to rise and fall. Quiet your mind and focus on your breath, relaxing any parts of you that are tight. Once your mind is quiet, picture in your mind the item, thing, or place from which you will be evoking. In your mind, introduce yourself, ask for permission to work with it, and see what response you imagine getting. If it is a feeling of rejection or even a vision or voice indicating "no," then stop immediately. The spirit does not want to work with you and you would be foolish and rude to pursue it. Most commonly you will get no response at all the first several times you do this, but eventually you will get an answer. When and if you get a "yes" answer, then proceed. The next several times that you meditate with the item, thing, or place, tell it more about yourself and why you want to work with it. When it feels right, ask it to show itself to you and to tell you about itself. Tell it about your needs, hopes, and, most important, your boundaries. Discuss them with the spirit to make sure that you both understand and respect each other's boundaries. Continue regularly meeting and talking with this spirit until you really feel like you have established a relationship. You can expect this process to take several months. If it takes less, then you are probably rushing it. It will almost certainly take the spirit a while to warm up to you. Nature spirits are very similar to wild animals in that regard. Just be patient, consistent, respectful, and persistent. If the spirit comes out and tells you to stop, do so. If it never shows you itself, tells you about itself, or otherwise seems less than friendly or cooperative, do not proceed. Possession by nature spirits can only be safely done when you both are working as a team. Listen to your intuition.

Archetypes

Once again, close your eyes and use your breath to become calm and relaxed. Picture in your mind the archetype or quality that you hope to eventually evoke. If your archetype is the Hunter, picture a mythic hunter, in whatever comes to mind. Perhaps you will see the Hunter dressed in animal furs, with hunting dogs, a bow, spear, and knife at hand. Or you might see the stereotypical safari hunter with pith helmet, khakis, and elephant rifle. If you will be working with a quality such as Courage or Strength, picture a person or thing exhibiting this quality. Once the image is clear in your mind's eye, introduce yourself to it. Tell it who you are and why you seek to work with it. Ask what its name is and if it would be willing to work with you. With archetypes, unlike nature spirits, who have distinct individual personalities, the answer will almost always be "yes." Keep dialoguing with the image, telling it about yourself, including your ethics and boundaries. Find out what it needs or wants. Be patient and respectful as you deal with this being. As with nature spirits, this process should take several months. You are building a relationship with another being, which takes time. If at any time your intuition tells you not to work with this being, listen.

Inner Divine Spark

Relax your mind and body. Once your mind is quiet, picture in your imagination a dark tunnel. This tunnel leads down into the core of your being. Follow the tunnel downward, moving ever deeper. As you travel you may see things from your life—fears, joys, experiences that made you who you are today. Just notice them and continue moving onward. They are not you or your core. This descending process might actually take several meditation sessions. Each time, just go as far as you can and then come back. The next time you should be able to jump to your last spot and continue on. Eventually, you will enter into a cave or other open space at the end of the tunnel. There, you will meet a radiant being. The being may look like a living fire, a person bathed in white light, a ball of white light, or something else entirely. Spend several more sessions just sitting with the Spark, soaking up what it feels like to be in contact with your deepest Self. When you feel ready, begin dialoguing with the Spark. Because it is your own core, you do not need to tell it who you are or why you are here, but just ask it what you need to know and how to work with it more closely. Ask it if it would be willing to be evoked to the surface. If so, ask it how it would like you to do so. Discuss with it your ethics and boundaries, your hopes and fears. This is very deep work and should take at least as long as the other evocable beings. As always, listen to your intuition and let it be your guide as to how much and how fast to open up.

Invocable Deities

After having done the research on the God or Goddess you hope to eventually evoke, the first step is to create an inviting environment. Many Gods and Goddesses have specific things they enjoy, such as flowers, incense, foods, and decorations, among other things. As much as is reasonable, try to create a setting that includes these things. Furthermore, if that God or Goddess is associated with a particular place, try to do your workings in that place. For example, Llyr, the Celtic ocean God, would best be worked with near the ocean. If that is not possible, perhaps having a seashell filled with seasalt on your altar will suffice.

Once the setting is in place, close your eyes and take a few moments to breathe. Feel your breath coming and going from your nostrils, causing your chest to rise and fall. Quiet your mind and focus on your breath, relaxing any parts of you that are tight. Once your mind is quiet, bring into your mind's eye an image of the God or Goddess. Picture every small detail from the type of clothes to the color of his or her eyes. Are there animals or other beings surrounding him or her? What is the setting—a forest, a glade, a Greek city? Bring your other senses into the meditation. Imagine the smells, the sounds, and the other feelings of being in that place and time with that God or Goddess.

Now bring that image forward in time to your ritual space and time. Imagine that God or Goddess there before you. Feel the Divine presence nearby. Introduce yourself and thank the God or Goddess for coming. Speak about yourself and why you have summoned him or her—to get better acquainted so as to see if this being is the right one for you to work with. Ask if he or she is willing to work with you. If you get the impression that the answer is "no," then apologize for any bother you have caused, thank the being for his or her time, and end the meditation. Do not bother the God or Goddess again. If the answer is "maybe" or "yes," then ask the the being you have summoned what he or she needs from you. Over the next several months, meditate with your God or Goddess. Discuss what your boundaries are and ask if he or she can work within them. Get to know your God or Goddess personally: likes, dislikes, and goals. You will be surprised to learn things about that you never get in books, such as specific tastes and preferences. If the being asks for offerings or oaths, do them if you feel like you can without compromising your integrity and values. Do not just do as asked because he or she is a deity. Only do it if it feels right to you and will build your relationship. You may eventually find that this God or Goddess is not right for you. If this happens, you will have to start the process all over again. It happens regularly, so do not be discouraged. When you find the right one, it will be worth the search.

Trance Induction

As mentioned earlier, the ability to enter the various levels of trance state can be very helpful in attaining the various levels of possession. A trance is not an absolute requirement for possession, nor do all such states involve possession, but they can be used to facilitate letting go and allowing the possession to happen.

There are two primary types of trance: inwardly focused and expansive. Inwardly focused states are those where, as the name implies, you keep narrowing your focus, moving deeper and deeper into your subconscious. Expansive states keep widening your focus and awareness to hold and include more things simultaneously. Let's try both of these before discussing them further.

Inwardly Focused Trance (Eyes Closed)

Find a comfortable place to sit or lie down. If you have a tendency to fall asleep when you close your eyes, then try sitting up. Begin by doing the deep relaxation and grounding and centering exercises from the first chapter. Quiet your body and mind. Focus on your breath. Feel it coming and going from your body. Notice how your chest rises and falls with each breath cycle. Pay attention to the feeling of your breath in your nostrils as it passes in and out. Feel your breath come in. Feel your breath go out. Notice the short pauses between your inhaling and exhaling. One pause is when your lungs are full, just before you exhale. The other pause is when your lungs are empty, just before your next inhale. Focus on that empty spot between your last exhale and your next inhale. Be aware of that moment. Focus on that moment for several minutes. With each breath cycle, as you focus on that empty moment, feel yourself moving deeper and deeper into the core of your being. After several more minutes, when you feel ready, start to come back out of your trance. Focus again on the whole breath cycle—the sensation of your breath in your nostrils. Feel your chest rise and fall with each breath. Become aware of your body as a whole, lying or sitting in your comfortable place. Become aware of the space around you. When you feel fully back to regular awareness, open your eyes. Come back feeling calm, relaxed, and energized.

Inwardly Focused Trance (Eyes Open)

Find a comfortable place to sit on a chair or the floor. Begin by doing the deep relaxation and grounding and centering exercises from the first chapter. Quiet your body and mind. Now direct your gaze toward a spot on the wall or floor. Ideally, the spot should be located about six feet away from you at a slight downward angle. It can be an actual mark or something on the wall or floor. I often find it easier to focus on a little part of the wood grain on the floor or one strand of the carpet piling. Or you can focus on an area without any features at all. Just pick a spot on a bare wall. Try it several ways and see what works best for you.

Once you've picked your spot, just gaze at it. Don't stare at it. Don't study it. Just be aware of it. Try not to notice or focus on anything else but the spot. This will take some work because your mind is going to want to wander, look around, think about things. But whenever you catch yourself starting to do those things, just bring your gaze back to your spot. Continue to gaze at your spot, refocusing your mind when it wanders, for fifteen to thirty minutes. When you are done, slowly bring your awareness to the floor or wall around the spot. Expand that awareness to the room and your body. When you are back, you should feel calm, relaxed, and invigorated. Practice this technique daily for several months. It will get easier as you continue, and you will notice that your focus becomes more intense and your conscious mind will temporarily shut down. Eventually, you will find that you can attain this level of focus at will almost immediately.

Expansive Trance

Find a place to sit that will be comfortable to stay in for a while. Ideally, this spot should be outdoors in nature, or at the very least, have a nice outdoor view. Do the deep relaxation and grounding and centering exercises from the first chapter. Quiet your body and mind. Now, with your eyes open, gaze at the scene before you. Try not to focus on any one thing. Try not to jump from thing to thing with your gaze either. Just take in the whole scene, without thought, judgment, or focusing. At first, you may find that this is challenging. Your natural instinct will be to jump from detail to detail, roaming the scene with your eyes. Your eyes will be naturally drawn to things that move, especially if there is sudden movement. But try to resist these urges. Just take in the whole scene simultaneously. Do this for fifteen to thirteen minutes a day until you can do it easily and in various settings. Then try taking in the whole scene while gradually expanding it to include your peripheral vision and even behind you. You will eventually be able to take in the whole 360 degrees around you. Once you have accomplished this, look farther away from your body and farther outside of your direct line of sight. This process can take a lifetime to master, so do not get discouraged if it is slow. Persistence will pay off.

Most techniques for trance induction fall into two types: sensory deprivation and overstimulation. Sensory deprivation techniques, like the trances just discussed, involve reducing outside sensory input so that there are no distractions to going into trance. Such techniques can range from relatively mild techniques such as the previous quiet meditations and focusing on natural sounds and sights to the use of various sensory-deprivation devices including flotation tanks and suspension harnesses. Generally, the more mild techniques are safer, but require repeated practice to work up to increasingly deeper trance states. Also, although the more extreme techniques can get someone deeper faster with less preparation, they tend to do the work of trance induction for the person. What this means is that for those who use devices to induce trance, they never learn to do it without the devices. A person who learns self-induction without anything but his or her breath often finds that he or she can eventually drop into trance at will any place and any time. This has its distinct advantages in ritual and life in general as the trance and possession states become more readily accessed at need, and let's face it, sometimes we need the advice or help of the Gods at times and places other than our formal rituals.

Overstimulation trance induction techniques are probably the most common worldwide. These techniques induce trance by providing too much stimulation for the mind. The mind is thus required to move into a deep focus to limit and moderate the amount of stimulation.

Overstimulation techniques exist for each of the five senses. For hearing, music, chanting, poetry, and drumming can be used. For vision, yantra, mandalas, spinning, and strobe lights, and "flashing colors" are common. For touch, the application of stimulating oils, various kinds of stroking, massaging and petting, feathers, whips, and other kinds of skin stimulation are used. Smell can be overstimulated by various heavy incenses and essential oils. Taste can also be overstimulated, most commonly with exceedingly hot foods and drinks but also with extremely bitter and sour tastes. Other overstimulation techniques include difficult yoga poses and mudras, ecstatic dance, Sufi twirling, and other types of repetitive movement.

It is common practice to combine several of these overstimulation techniques together. Thus, a person might eat some hot peppers, apply a mint oil to his or her body to create contrast with the hot food, burn some myrrh and frankincense, turn on the strobe lights, and begin chanting while he or she dances to a tape of drumming. Or he or she might chant while gazing at a mandala, all the while holding a difficult yoga posture. The possibilities are almost endless. Pretty much any activity that requires a high degree of focus, which can also include such common things as creating artwork, rock climbing, and juggling, can be used to induce trance.

Similar to the sensory-deprivation techniques, overstimulation techniques can be used for both types of trance. A repetitive dance where one closes his or her eyes and stays in one place will tend to create an inwardly focused trance, whereas dancing in a group of people where everyone is circling a bonfire will tend to expand your focus so that you don't bump into other people or things. It all comes down to your intention and what you need to do to trance. If the technique requires you to focus on some small detail to maintain it, then it is probably an inwardly focused induction. If it requires you to see an ever-widening picture to maintain the trance, then it is probably an expansive induction.

Techniques for Provoking Possession

As we have seen, there are different types of trance: inwardly focused and expansive. Those trance states can be induced by both sensory deprivation and overstimulation techniques. Within those trance states, there are several stages of trance ranging from simply enhancement of one's own awareness and power to deep states of full deity possession. Then, one's theological model will determine the nature of the Divine that is being contacted and whether evocation or invocation is required.

Evocation is the calling of a God, Goddess, or spirit out of one's self or some item, place, or thing. Because this is a "calling out," it only makes sense that this requires an inwardly focused trance state to contact that inwardly dwelling being.

Drawing Out a Nature Spirit

Find a tree or plant with which you would like to commune. Do extensive research on all the properties and folklore associated with this plant. Make certain that you have a guardian with you to help open and close the ritual, keep an eye on your safety, and care for you after you are back.

Burn a good-quality incense that appeals to you. If the tree or plant you will be working with has an incense, such as pine or cedar, that would be ideal. Stare at the plant until you have every little piece of the image clearly in your mind. Touch the plant, smell it, and perhaps even taste it. Hold these in your mind as you close your eyes and begin to chant the sound "hoom." Begin to gently rock back and forth as you continue your visualization and chant. Do this for several minutes until your intuition tells you that you have done it enough. Then ask the plant to show you a form of its spirit. You will either see this with your mind's eye, or you might actually see it optically. This is the being with which you will begin your dialogue about ethics. Have this dialogue and once it is done, thank the being and return to normal consciousness.

For the next several sessions, you will want to do the induction and once the spirit is contacted, continue this dialogue. After several dialoging sessions, assuming that you and the spirit have agreed to work together, your ethical boundaries have been clearly set, and you are confident that the spirit will honor them, during your next trance ritual ask the spirit to lend you its energy or qualities for a few minutes. Feel the power flow into and through you. This is the enhancement stage.

After a few sessions experiencing the enhancement stage, come up with a problem that you need help with and ask the spirit to lend you its power, wisdom, and insight for a few minutes. When the spirit does so, you will feel the power come in, but you will also start to pick up images, visions, feelings, and occasionally even a voice giving you advice and inspiration. This is the inspiration stage and is typically the highest level of evocation of an entity outside of yourself. To go deeper would mean to bring the spirit into your body, at which point we have switched to invocation.

Drawing Out a God or Goddess Archetype

This same evocation technique can be used to bring the Divine up out of your core. As before, make certain that you have a guardian with you to help open and close the ritual, keep an eye on your safety, and care for you after you are back.

Before you begin this ritual, have within your ritual space items with which to make a mask. These might include some stiff paper for a backing, string to tie it on with, and then various paints, glitter, leaves, sticks, pictures, pieces of fabric, or whatever strikes your fancy. You will also need scissors to cut eyeholes and trim things, plus glue to attach the various items. Don't forget to have old newspapers and paper towels around to prevent permanent messes in your ritual space.

To begin the ritual, create your sacred space as usual. Burn an incense that you find deepens your meditations. Frankincense, jasmine, and sandalwood are good choices. Have your guardian drum or put on a drumming tape and begin to move slowly and carefully in a rhythmic fashion. Feel your mind drop away and move deeper and deeper into trance. When you feel right, imagine your awareness dropping downward into the core of your very self, to that Divine spark you met in an earlier exercise. When you have contacted this being, ask it to inspire your creativity to make a mask of its power. While holding that request in your mind, with the drumming still going on in the background, open your eyes and begin to create a mask. Follow your inspiration. When you are done, ask the being to imbue the mask with some of its power. Thank the being and return to normal consciousness. In the future, whenever you put on the mask, particularly in ritual settings, you will feel the power of your inner Divine fill you. This is the enhancement stage.

After working with the power of enhancement for a while, when you are in ritual wearing the mask, ask the being to provide you with further insight and inspiration. You will begin to see, hear, feel, and just know things that you would not normally experience. This is the inspiration stage. Practice being able to tap into this inspiration at will, with or without the mask.

When your intuition tells you that you are ready, while wearing the mask in trance ritual with your guardian present, open yourself up to letting the spirit gradually have control of your body. This is not invocation because you are not bringing something in from outside. This is still evocation because you are bringing something from the inside to the outside. However, when you finally feel another consciousness in your body, then you are in the integration stage. With practice, as you continue to let go of control, you will move toward deeper and deeper levels of possession.

As mentioned earlier, invocation is the calling of a God, Goddess, or spirit that is outside of yourself into your body. Depending on your theological model, this can require either an inwardly focused trance state or an expansive trance state.

If you are a nontheist, panentheist, or a pantheist who doesn't believe in any type of personified deity, then you are more likely to seek an expansive trance state. That is, if what you are seeking to invoke is the Tao, the All, enlightened Oneness with all things, then what you want to do is to expand your consciousness to include everything. However, if you are a polytheist or pantheist who works with specific aspects of the God and Goddess, then you will want a focused trance state that will zoom in specifically on that deity or aspect of deity and bring that into yourself. Think of it as a sort of psychic tractor-beam to the Gods.

The quintessential expansive invocation was given in an earlier exercise. You simply keep expanding your awareness and folding it back into yourself. So let's look at a Wiccan-style inwardly focused invocation.

Drawing Down a God or Goddess

Earlier, you were directed to pick a God or Goddess, do some research, and begin to dialogue with that deity so as to establish a relationship and your ethical boundaries. So just as you did then, again create your ritual setting with incenses, sounds, and images appropriate for the deity. These, along with your breath and concentration, will serve to focus your trance state. Have your guardian create sacred space. Once the setting is in place, close your eyes and take a few moments to breathe. Feel your breath coming and going from your nostrils, causing your chest to rise and fall. Quiet your mind and focus on your breath, relaxing any parts of you that are tight. Once your mind is quiet, bring into your mind's eye an image of the God or Goddess. As you have in the past, picture every small detail about that deity, his or her setting and companions. From your prior work, you should be able to bring that deity alive in your mind. You should be able to feel the presence of that God or Goddess around you. You have already accomplished the enhancement state. And because you have been dialoguing with this deity, you have also mastered the inspiration state. You didn't even realize that you were half way there, did you? Keep practicing invoking the presence of this deity and asking him or her for inspiration and information.

Eventually, your intuition will tell you that you are ready to begin carrying. This time after your trance induction, spend several moments just letting go of control of your body. Imagine yourself as an empty vessel. Invite the spirit to enter your body. You may have to try this several times before you are able to let go of control of yourself to let this happen, but eventually you will feel the spirit enter you. You have entered the integration stage. And with practice, as you become more comfortable with the spirit in your body and get better at letting go, you will move further and further into possession trance. At first, you will feel like you have two people in your body, with them occasionally switching who has control of your motor functions and speech. As you continue to relinquish control, the deity will gain increasing control over your body and words. When you come back, you may or may not remember what you said or did, or you may only remember parts. Those blank spots are when the God or Goddess was in complete control. This can be a bit scary, which is why you have a guardian present to make sure that when you are gone and only the deity is in control, your boundaries and safety are maintained.

Once you accomplish a full possession, then you have a few options. If you are a polytheist or monotheist, you will want to invoke your particular deity regularly and often to attune yourself more closely to his or her will and to make the process easier and more fluid. As with most things, practice makes things easier and more automatic.

If you are a pantheist, then the fun begins. You can begin invoking a variety of deities with whom you have an interest in working. As always, do the research and dialoguing first. Don't just invoke deities at random or you might not like what you get. And even if you get the God or Goddess you want, you might not always expect how he or she will respond. Several years ago I invoked the God of the Forests as part of a ritual. The plan was for the God to then speak to the assembled group and to give specific advice to people with questions for the God. The only problem was that the God of the Forest, being a God of animals and trees, is not a "people-person." So for the entire ritual, he just sat there silently watching the ritual and people with a sense of amusement. The part of me that was drawn down thought that was very funny. The part of me that had planned the ritual was mortified with the awkward silence. In the end, because no one was saying anything, the ritual participants were forced to silently focus inward themselves and it turned into a powerful ritual in its own right. But it wasn't how we had originally planned it. So be aware that the Gods don't always follow the script.

Another educational thing to do is to invoke both male and female deities regardless of your gender. To feel the consummate force of femininity in your male body gives you a whole new understanding and appreciation for the other sex and makes you acutely aware of the limits of your gender identification. That is, if you have a strong identification as, for example, a heterosexual male, you may find your self-identity challenged when the Goddess in you is attracted to another male. And after you are particularly skilled in invocation, and you are feeling a little adventurous, try invoking two or more lover deities simultaneously into your body. When the two cosmic forces of male and female, of yin and yang, of God and Goddess meet in one body, it can be extremely powerful and intense. Ecstatic doesn't begin to describe it, nor can words capture it. You'll have to try it yourself.

Finally, once you have mastered evocation and invocation yourself, you will find that you can help to induce trance and possession in other people. You will know the techniques and guideposts to help assist them in their own learning and experiences.

How to Care for Someone During and After Possession

During possession, the guardian is responsible for keeping the ritual going, keeping the invoked person safe, and ensuring that the deity keeps the prearranged boundaries. Be nearby, but do not interact or interfere unless asked to by the person or deity or unless the person is moving into unsafe territory. Some people will be fully mobile while possessed. Others will fall to the floor and either lie very still, or convulse violently. If they are lying still, cover their body to help keep them warm. A deep trance state will drop the person's body temperature. People won't notice it while in trance, but when they come back, they will be freezing. If the person is convulsing or crying, you may want to gently hold him or her. Do not restrain the person and do not speak. Just provide the physical support so that no harm is done. Do not get anxious for the ritual to end. Let the trance run its course. Although I have heard stories of people getting lost and unable to return to their bodies, I have never actually seen nor experienced anyone not coming back from trance possession. So let the trance run its course. It may be fifteen minutes or fifteen hours. As guardian, you have to commit to riding it out with the person you are guarding.

Once the person has come back, he or she may be cold, hungry, stiff, and disoriented. Keep the person wrapped in warm clothes and provide food and water. Hearty, filling, and nutritional foods tend to ground and nurture people more than sugar and caffeine. Massage the person so that he or she can come fully back into the body. When the person is ready, help with walking and stretching, and taking deep breaths to wake back up. Keep checking in with the person until he or she seems to be back to normal functioning. Do not let people drive home until it is safe for them to do so.

Divine possession is some of the most advanced and powerful work that a Wiccan can do. With that power comes great responsibility. It is important that you do this work carefully and with due respect. Take the time to truly master the techniques. Do not rush the process and do not skip steps. Work with the Gods *will* change you and your world. Your attitude and approach will determine how gentle or brutal those changes will be.

CHAPTER 8

Mastery: Living the Magickal Life

The work of an adept is transformation. As you have progressed through the preceding chapters, you have learned many things about being an adept. He or she is skilled in magick and energy and understands how those skills can be used to transform reality. An adept is knowledgeable about how energy is influenced by will and intention, and uses that knowledge to create around him- or herself an environment suitable for further growth and change. Well grounded in a diversity of skills and knowledge, the adept has stopped rote performance of ritual and instead is flexible and able to adapt and customize the workings based on that deeper knowledge and experience. Through intuition and clairvoyance, an adept is aware of the patterns, pulse, and flow of the Divine will as well as other influences acting on his or her life.

Being attuned to the outside forces of the seasons and nature and the inside forces operating in the adept's own body enables harmonization with them and transformation to a life of balance, fulfillment, and health. The adept understands how spiritual and personal growth and transformation work and, in accord with the Divine will, uses that understanding to bring change and development within and to those around him- or herself. Finally, through a strong connection with the Divine, an adept becomes

223

a vehicle for the Divine will of the Gods to manifest and transform the world. The goal of this book has been to transform you the reader into this kind of adept.

And yet, this book is also about magickal living. As we defined it in chapter 1, magickal living is a state of being instead of a state of doing. Magickal living is living in harmony with the will of the Divine, attuned to the flow of nature's cycles and energies. More than anything, the work of an adept is the transformation of self. By living consciously and magickally, a witch transforms the world not by what he or she does or knows but by who he or she is.

Close your eyes and clear your mind. Fully relax your body, letting any tension from the day drain out of you. When you are ready, picture yourself sitting in an inner tube or small inflatable raft that is floating down a gentle, calm little river. It is a beautiful and sunny day. Hear the lapping of the water around you, the song of birds in the trees on the riverbank, and the buzz of insects in the nearby grass. Feel the warmth of the sun and the coolness of the water as the small currents and eddies of the river gently rock you. All is calm, peaceful, and comfortable.

As you float down the river, you find yourself becoming more and more aware of the subtleties of the river's flow. You start to notice places where the water moves faster and slower. You also notice that some currents come near to boulders in the river, some smash directly into the rocks, and some avoid the rocks altogether. There are deep places in the river and spots where it is so shallow that your tube scrapes on the bottom and you have to use your hands and feet to push yourself through. If you just let the river take you as it will, you may have an easy, peaceful ride, or you may find yourself having to work very hard your whole ride and never get very far. Or worse, you may end up dashed on the rocks. Most likely you'll get a little of each.

Being in the tube, you also notice that you have some control over where the river takes you. At first, you try to drive your tube by kicking and paddling aggressively. That helps some, and certainly helps to avoid the major crashes, but it is hard work and you still find yourself occasionally stuck or bashed.

Eventually, you notice that just by making small adjustments with your hands and feet, using them more as rudders than paddles, you have more control. You also find that the more you are aware of the subtle river currents, the easier it is to pick the right ones to get you where you want to go and avoid the rocks. As you become more attuned to the river, you have to do less steering, making only occasional slight adjustments with your feet and hands. The journey begins to become effortless. You become peaceful and harmonious again.

Most people go through life like the tuber on the river. Many simply allow the currents and tides of life to carry them as it will. Some of them get an easy, prosperous ride through life. Others get scarred and battered as they drag themselves from day to day, just trying to survive. Some do not make it all.

Some people refuse to accept that they are at the mercy of the river of life. They try to find ways to work with or overcome the obstacles set before them. Some of these people decide to take the path of their lives into their own hands. Some barter with God by praying daily and trying to make deals so that the river will be kind. Others attempt to force their own will and designs on the river of life by, manipulating people, things, and events as best as they can. They break through the rocks and redirect the river with some success. Life can appear good for a while. But it is a lot of work to combat the river. The river is seemingly endless and eternal. Eventually, even the hardiest, strongest willed person succumbs.

But Witches and Pagans are magickal people. We know that life and nature *are* the Divine. The very act of living is a sacred act, whether or not we "go with the flow" or fight life screaming and kicking all the way. Our only choice is how we are going to live our lives. People who are adept at magickal living have made the conscious decision to become the gentle steersman of the meditation. They seek to become more aware of the subtle currents and energies in their lives and by doing so empower themselves to have the journey through life that they want.

At this point you might ask: How can I recognize an adept when I meet one and how will I know when I have reached that level? The short answer is: If you have been doing the exercises in this book, you will know. Your intuition, awareness, and connection to the Divine will all tell you. You can be certain, however, that adepts are not recognizable by any superficial signs. The color of their robes, the number of degrees they have, students they've trained, or books they've written all have no bearing on whether or not they really are an adept. Many of the ones I know own no robes and their ritual tools are simple household items. I know adepts who hold advanced college degrees and those who never finished high school. They can be child-like with braids to their ankles or dour curmudgeons. Many times they are the ones with the t-shirt and unkempt hair at the festival. They quietly observe and guide in an almost invisible manner. A gentle suggestion here. An idea dropped there. They are always assisting in moving the energy and working with the spirits in subtle, unobtrusive ways. People often underestimate them or don't notice them at all as they rush to be with the person with the flashiest robes, the most regal bearing, and the largest number of groupies.

And yet, there are clues that give them away. Some clues are very subtle. There is a depth and wisdom in their eyes. There is an easy, peaceful balance to their lives. They are the people who get things done at a festival or ritual without seeking credit. They are dependable and consistent. They have lives that work. The well-known Pagans whose personal lives are always a drama and who can't seem to hold a job are not adepts. Other clues are not so subtle. When the small, frail, quiet, elder at the edge of the circle suddenly becomes a seven-foot, beautiful, powerful, and somewhat frightening Goddess who cuts to the heart of an issue and tells you exactly what you have to hear, you are in the presence of an adept. Whether you notice them or not, they are always there.

In the preceding chapters, you were presented with a wide array of definitions, concepts, exercises, meditations, and rituals with which to work. If you actually do these exercises, you *will* become an adept. There could easily be years of study and practice there. For myself, I've read some fantastic books loaded with recommended readings, crafty projects, rituals, meditations, and other spiritual exercises not too dissimilar to the one in your hand. However, it quickly became evident that unless I gave up everything else in my life—my job, family, friends, coven work, and maybe even sleeping—then there was no way that I could realistically do everything in those books. The study programs in those books were fantastic in theory, but in practice were unrealistic. And so those books sit on my shelf and most of the exercises go undone. The real question then, the one that pertains most directly to the idea of living a magickal life, is: So now that I have all of this information, how do I apply it in my everyday life?

The way to apply these new skills and to begin living a magickal life is to begin practicing daily magick and gradually start to transform yourself and your life. The following is a list of small things that you can do every day to start living magickally:

1. Ground and center at least once a day. Many people find it useful to ground and center on awaking and then again at the end of the day just before going to bed. In the morning, grounding and centering helps you to wake you up and focus your mind for the tasks ahead. At the end of the day, it helps to clear any lingering tension or feelings from the day so that you get a good night's sleep.

2. Create ritual space daily, perhaps right after your morning grounding and centering. Doing this daily accomplishes two things. First, it makes you do some kind of magick every day. It is like any other skill, if you don't use it, you get rusty. So by doing daily magick, you keep your skills

fresh and your energy flowing. Second, we saw earlier how creating ritual space requires that you be mindful of your intent and the energetic environment around you. By performing daily ritual, you are giving yourself the opportunity to practice being aware of the currents and energies in your life. Only by knowing what they are can you hope to harmonize them with the Divine will and live a magickal life.

3. While in your ritual space, take a moment to bring in some energy through Qi Gong or one of the other exercises and allow it to course through your body. Heal yourself of any blockages or deficiencies you have. When you are in harmony in your body, your energy flows better and you are more open to Divine inspiration.

4. Keep a calendar marked out with the Wheel of the Year including the full and new moons. Be sure to include any of the mythic cycles that speak to you. Then every day before you start your regular day, look at your calendar. Notice what natural cycles and forces are in play and think about how your plans for the day reflect, compliment, or conflict with those forces. If possible, modify your plans to be more in harmony with the Wheel.

5. Practice your intuition every chance you get. It is one of the major keys to understanding the will of the Divine. Once developed, it will never lead you wrong. So make sure to consciously use your intuition at least once a day. Ideally, you will use it continually all day, everyday.

In addition, you may want to try these steps at least once a month:

1. Take some time to reflect on ways in which you can continue to learn and grow. Make a plan of study and then do a dedication ritual committing yourself to it. Then every month review your progress. Once you have accomplished your goal, do an achievement initiation as described in

chapter 6 and move onto the next stage. The goal should be to continually move into greater and great harmony and attunement with the Divine will.

2. Once a month practice trance, invocation, and evocation. By working directly with the Divine, however we conceptualize it, we better attune ourselves to the Divine plan and open ourselves up to more profound intuition and deeper insight.

By focusing at least once a day on watching the currents of life and trying to bring balance and harmony with those currents into your life, you will gradually find that you are becoming adept. In the beginning, it will seem deceptively easy. But if you are truly doing these exercises and not just reading them, transformation will start to happen. And transformation can be traumatic. As you become more aware and attuned, those people, possessions, and activities in your life that are unhealthy for you will start to fall away. They can do so in very dramatic and unsettling ways. At some point you may feel like your whole life is falling apart — and it will be. Terror and transformation — the dark night of the soul. The old has to be washed out before the new can begin.

If you hold steady and continue to live magickally by reconnecting with your intuition and attuning to the Divine, you *will* make it through. Gradually, you will notice new, more nurturing, and healthy people and events coming into your life. Life will become less effort. Your intuition will keep you informed so that you just know what to do, when to do it, and how. You will find that you have skill, knowledge, and awareness, so much so that at the same moment that you realize you want or need something, that something will "magickally" appear. The level of your attunement to the forces and flow of nature will give you the power to create positive change without appearing to do anything. You will find yourself transformed and deeply connected to and in harmony with the will of the Gods. You will be an adept Wiccan practitioner. So mote it be.

PAGAN RESOURCES

Books

Alexandria. *Wiccan Feng Shui: How to Arrange a Magickal Life*. New York: Citadel Press, 2002.

Coyle, Thorn. *Evolutionary Witchcraft*. New York: Jeremy P. Tarcher/Penguin, 2004.

Grey Cat. *Deepening Witchcraft: Advanced Skills and Knowledge*. Toronto, Canada: ECW Press, 2002.

Landry, Forrest. "The Immanent Metaphysics." Private Publication. www.uvsm.com.

McCoy, Edain. *Advanced Witchcraft: Go Deeper, Reach Further, Fly Higher*. St. Paul, MN: Llewellyn, 2004.

Vaughan, Frances. *Awakening Intuition*. Garden City, NY: Anchor Books, 1979.

Web Sites

Ardantane, www.ardantane.org.

Cherry Hill Seminary, www.cherryhillseminary.org.

Kirk White's Home Page, www.revkirkwhite.com.

INDEX

ABOUT THE AUTHOR

KIRK WHITE has been a practicing witch for nearly thirty years. The past director of the University of Vermont's Parapsychology Program, he founded two Pagan organizations: the Wiccan Church of Vermont and the Church of the Sacred Earth: A Union of Pagan Congregations. A longtime teacher of courses in Wicca and witchcraft, White is also the founder, president, and academic dean of Cherry Hill Seminary (www.cherryhillseminary.com), a professional Pagan clergy education program. The author lives at Laurelin (www.laurelincommunity.com), a fifty-acre Pagan spiritual retreat in Vermont with his wife, Amy, and their daughter, Killian. More information is available at his Web site, www.revkirkwhite.com.